# CAFECITO

# CAFECITO

SHYSEL GRANADOS

NEW DEGREE PRESS

COPYRIGHT © 2021 SHYSEL GRANADOS

*All rights reserved.*


CAFECITO


ISBN    978-1-63730-834-9    *Paperback*
         978-1-63730-898-1    *Kindle Ebook*
         978-1-63730-953-7    *Ebook*

# TABLE OF CONTENTS

# MI NOMBRE

I've grown accustomed to seeing my name underlined in red on Word documents and the like. Having spellcheck "correct" my name, "Shysel" to "chisel" because that's what it thought I was trying to spell. I love my name, but it has been burdensome.

My mom named me after her best friend from high school. It's French, and that's all I know. I've asked my mom about my name so many times over the years, but she truly has no other information to share with me. I've looked up my name online, and to my disappointment, nothing—or at least no one with internet familiarity or knowledge of how to post online about my name.

I've even tried looking for French names but no luck. Zip. Zilch. Nada. Google Translate, you have failed me.

Shysel is pronounced *chee-sel*, but, unfortunately, it wasn't easy for the other kids to pronounce. Some kids didn't try to learn, and one went as far as bullying me. I was in second grade, and I remember it got so bad that one morning, I refused to go to school. I threw a fit, I cried, and I wouldn't tell Mami what happened. Mami patiently waited for me to calm down and asked why I didn't want to go. When I did tell her, we walked to school, she talked to the administration and my teacher, and they settled the matter. My teacher then acted as mediator while my bully and I discussed why I was upset, how my feelings were hurt, and how we could move forward. He apologized, and he stopped making fun of my name…mostly.

There was another incident in fourth grade when another classmate chose to single me out because of my name. He twisted it into something ugly and disgusting that I do not wish to repeat today. Based on my past experiences, I ignored him and did not encourage his antics. Over time, he slowly stopped, but still called me X every once in a while.

Every time he called me hurtful names, there was a pain in my chest as if someone had shoved me to the ground and spit on my face. I was confused by his taunting; I gave him no reason to bully me, and yet, he felt pleasure in making fun of my name. I never told my teacher or Mami about his hurtful antics or how it felt to be called something else rather than my name.

Incidents like that made me feel so self-conscious about my name that I even considered changing it; but then I met more people who would compliment it, saying how unique and pretty it was. It made me feel better and more confident in my name. I felt a sense of pride in carrying the name Shysel.

Despite the compliments, I continued to introduce myself as "Seashell" in school and work environments to make things easier. I avoid having to pronounce Shysel because there is a voice inside me saying, *They're not going to say it right. Don't bother. Make it easier on them. Just say Seashell.* And I do.

"My name is Seashell."

"Say it again please."

I enunciate, "Sea-shell."

"Sea-shell?"

I nod.

"Like she sells seashells—"

I laugh at the reference I've heard since fifth grade. "Yes, down by the seashore."

"That's so pretty!"

"Thank you!"

At home, my family and childhood friends call me Chio (pronounced *chee-o*). One of my childhood best friends claims she came up with my nickname, but Mami says my older brother had difficulty in pronouncing my name, so he came up with Chio. And it stuck. Almost everyone in my close circle calls me Chio.

Another nickname I go by is Chel (pronounced *chi-l*), but the only people who call me that are my cousins y Tío Martin. Their mom, Tía Rocio, switches between Chio and Chel. Personally, I love that they are the only ones who call me Chel. It's endearing and familiar.

Sometimes, when my family and school life mix, it's a little weird to have my parents call me Chio around my friends, but that's only because my friends know me as Seashell. It's not that I'm a different person, not entirely at least, but because they are getting to see a whole other side to me.

Seashell is a hardworking, determined student who actively participates in class, turns in her work (mostly) on time, and helps her classmates with homework and projects. Seashell is a team player who engages in meetings, listens to her supervisors, and jokes with her coworkers.

Chio and Chel are a daughter, the peacemaker in the family. Just like Seashell, Chio is devoted to her family, but she can be loud, *exagerada*, and passionate. She will joke and laugh with her siblings, help her parents with grocery shopping, and occasionally get into trouble—especially with her friends.

Chio helps her younger siblings with their homework, washes dishes, cleans the cat's litter box, and watches movies with her family. Chio loves to paint alongside her sister and show her parents the end result. She is kind, soft, and strong willed but still learning to be confident in her voice.

In the beginning, there was very little overlap between Seashell and Chio, but as the years went by, they've slowly merged closer together. Depending on the setting (school presentation, meeting with supervisors, *una fiesta con la familia*, hanging out with my family, etc.), either Seashell or Chio would be the forerunner, and the other one takes the baton when needed.

That is not to say either is incomplete or inauthentic; they are two sides of the same coin.

Recently, my boyfriend adopted one of the names my parents use: Shysel. When my boyfriend first heard them call me Shysel, he asked me how to say it and practiced saying it over and over again, until it became familiar and comfortable in his mouth, like waves smoothing out rocks on the beach.

"Say it again slowly."

"Chee-"

"Chee-" he repeats after me.

"-sel."

"-sel."

"Chee-sel."

"Shysel?" he asks.

I nod. "Shysel."

He smiles. "Shysel."

Eventually, he stopped using Seashell and began using Shysel regularly. And I love it. He took time, effort, and great care to learn how to say my name like my parents do. When he says my name, it gives me a warm, comforting feeling and reminds me of home. This small act of care is one of the reasons why I'm in love with him. He chose to learn and continues to call me Shysel, no matter the situation.

When we moved in together, he called me Shysel in front of our roommates; when we are hanging out with our friends, he calls me Shysel; when he introduces me to someone new, he calls me Shysel; he will call me Shysel every time. He enunciates every syllable to ensure he says it correctly to everyone.

Despite the burdens I have had with my name, I carry it proudly and with love. Those who truly care about me will say it with love and care. My name is a part of my identity, just as Seashell and Shysel are the same person. A team player, a hard worker, and a devoted daughter and sister.

*Me llamo* Shysel.

# CAFÉ CON MIS PADRES

I remember drinking my first cup of coffee at around age ten. I was in elementary school, and it was a weekend morning. As per usual, Papi had gone to *el panaderia* to buy *pan dulce por el café*, and Mami prepped the table with plates, jams, and cottage cheese to top our *pan dulce*.

By that point, Papi y Mami had let me try their coffee black before, and it was horrible. Little me was perplexed as to why adults didn't like sweet stuff, but they liked weird, bitter, plain flavors.

"Mami, why do you drink *café*?" I asked her one morning. "It tastes gross."

She served me a half cup and handed me a spoon and creamer.

"Here, try this."

I added some creamer, stirred it, and took a cautious sip.

*Not bad.* I then added a little more creamer and took a bigger sip.

"See? It's better," Mami said with a smile as I drank more.

"Now try it *con pan!*" Papi enthusiastically handed me a *concha de chocolate*.

I tore off a piece, dipped it in my coffee, and took a bite. It was delicious, and I immediately went for more.

Papi laughed.

From that day forward, I would drink a cup of coffee every Sunday with my parents.

For as long as I can remember, we had *pan dulce con café* every weekend. Usually in the spring and summer, we added a fruit platter to our brunch. No matter what, there was always *pan dulce* on the table, baked fresh that morning from our local *panaderia*. Even if we had brunch at our cousins or *con los vecinos*, Papi made sure to bring *pan por el café*.

My siblings and I loved going with Papi to choose from the selection, for our family and ourselves. As young kids, we usually got the slice of yellow cake with white frosting, a thin layer of red jam in the middle, and colorful sprinkles on top. It was our favorite, although most of the time we only ate the bit with the frosting and jam.

Mami's favorite, and Fluffy's (my nickname for my sister Sherlyn), was *el porquito*: it has a soft, crumbly texture vaguely shaped like a pig and colored brown. Another of their favorites was *pan de muerto*, a soft, kind of dense and fluffy at the same time, bread decorated at the top with sprinkled granulated sugar and little trimmings at the top. *Pan de muerto* is typically made for *Día de los Muertos* and placed on *el ofrenda* or even the tombstone of your loved one as a treat for their soul to munch on after their long journey to our world.

Mami also loved *el pan de piña*. It was similar to a Danish pastry but filled with pineapple filling *and* cream cheese. It was a long, rectangular flaky pastry, with some slashes at the top to display the pineapple filling. It became one of my favorites as well.

Mami and Fluffy would sometimes argue over *el porquito y pan de muerto*.

Fluffy served herself some coffee and grabbed a plate. She walked over to the platter and reached for *el pan de muerto*.

"No, no, no," Mami said as she spread jam on her toast. "That's for me."

Fluffy huffed and reached for *el porquito.*

"That one is for me too."

Exasperated, Fluffy grabbed *el pan de piña* and—

"That one too."

Fluffy dropped *el pan de piña,* grabbed *el porquito,* walked over to Mami, and broke it in half. She placed one piece on Mami's plate.

"There. That's for you."

Mami took a sip of her coffee and smiled. *"Gracias, mija."*

Papi's favorites included *el pan de piña, conchas y los cuernos.* The *conchas* came in two different flavors, *vainilla y chocolate.* They were made with the same base: a dense, slightly airy bread topped with a crumbly sugar topping shaped to mimic the lining of a seashell (*conchas* are my go-to and never fail to make me smile. My brothers and I *love* these). He also loves *el pan de muerto y el porquito.* Truth be told, he loves them all, but he'll always have *un cuerno con su champurrado o café* no matter what.

Papi will always get *cuernos blanco y de mantequilla,* as well as *conchas* because they pair so well *con café y champurrado. Los cuernos* are shaped like croissants but are not flaky. *Los cuernos blanco* are lighter and airier, a little simple for my taste but still good. *Los cuernos de mantequilla* are the buttery, slightly dense cousins *de los cuernos blancos* (personally, *los cuernos blanco* pair better *con champurrado y los cuernos de mantequilla* go best *con Chocolate de Abuelita*).

And every year in January, we get *el Rosca de Reyes* from *el Panaderia México. El Rosca de Reyes* translates to "King's Wreath," and it is served on *Día de Reyes,* or "Three King's Day." In Mexico, *Día de Reyes* is celebrated on the sixth of

January, twelve days after Christmas (as it is believed), when the Three Kings visited baby Jesus.

Although I don't particularly love the flavor of *el Rosca de Reyes*, I still love it due to its sentimental value and the memories it holds for me.

*El Rosca de Reyes* is shaped like a wreath: a yellow bread adorned with candied fruit meant to represent the jewels on a king's crown. It is usually a plain bread, flavored with some citrus to give it a little flavor and pairs well *con champurrado y chocolate*. Historically, a small porcelain or tin figurine of a baby is hidden somewhere in the bread, waiting to be found. Nowadays, it is a small plastic figurine, and three are placed randomly within the bread.

Here's the kicker: you don't want the baby to be found in your piece. You can cut a small, thin slice or a big, chunky slice to eat, but you must avoid getting the baby. If the baby is found in your slice, you are chosen to host a dinner party for everyone (traditionally, *tamales* are served at the party).

My family usually joined our neighbors for the cutting of *el Rosca de Reyes*, gathering about their table, everyone waiting for their turn anxiously, hoping all three babies are found before their turn. That's what makes it so hilarious: you never know where the babies are, so everyone is stabbing and poking their slices to ensure the baby isn't there and some people like to cut thick slices, putting everyone on edge.

One year, I remember trying to cut myself a small slice to avoid the baby.

"¡*Ay, no* Shysel!" My neighbor, Simon, grabbed another knife and cut himself a thick slice. "¡*Necesitas un pedazo grande!*"

He then proceeded to cut his slice lengthwise to ensure he didn't get the baby. Everyone craned their necks to see. He held open his slice proudly.

I stood there shocked and proud of his slice.

"You got lucky!" my *tío* Luis yelled.

Simon laughed and dunked his slice into his *champurrado*.

Or in some cases, a family member, usually the nosy person, will even grab your slice and break apart the bread to ensure you don't have the baby.

My sister had just finished slicing her piece when our *tío*, Javier, snatched it from her.

He sliced it lengthwise and opened it. He even poked the bread!

"*¡No te pasas*, Javier!" Mami snatched back the piece and handed it back to Fluffy. "She's still gonna eat it!"

*Tío* Javier smiled and shrugged. "You never know!"

Fluffy walked away from *Tío* Javier and sat next to Mami as she ate her piece.

Kids participate in the cutting as well, increasing their parents' chance of being future host.

Another year, one of the neighbor's kids, Juan, came by to join the fun and eat some food.

The hosts allowed him to slice a piece, and he excitedly participated. He was around five years old and loved the attention everyone gave him. Simon grabbed his slice and proceeded to cut it lengthwise.

"Did he get it?" one of the parents asked.

Simon stopped cutting about halfway and smiled. He tore open the piece and pulled out the baby.

The crowd went wild.

Some of the dads gave Juan a high five and a pat on the back while Juan giggled and shrieked with joy. He grabbed the baby and began to show it off to everyone.

One of the moms took photos.

"So that his mom knows she has to cook for everyone," she explained to the others. They all laughed.

It's a great time: everyone laughing and yelling, people contemplating how big of a slice (read: risk) they want to take, the exaggeration of cutting a slice, everyone leaning in to see if there is a baby, making sure no one is hiding their baby, and just egging each other to cut a bigger slice.

It's one of my favorite celebrations.

Now that I've moved out of my parents' house and live with my boyfriend, Jah, I try to spend a weekend every now and then with my family *por café y pan dulce*. I still go to *el panaderia con* Papi to select *los panes*, turn on the coffee machine, prep the table, and wake up the family. Sometimes we'll watch a movie while we eat, but more often than not, everyone starts talking and joking with one another and the movie becomes part of the background.

As I sit there, sipping *mi café* and eating my *concha*, and listen to Mami and Fluffy banter while my brothers laugh *con* Papi, I feel full—full of love and gratitude to be able to enjoy *mi café con pan* with my family on a Sunday morning.

Our simple weekly ritual of having *pan con café* is a comfort and holds a special place in my heart. Despite how often it occurs or the simplicity of it all, it remains special because we are all together. Even on the mornings when one of us is sleeping in or Papi is working, we save their favorite *pan* so they can come back and enjoy it *con café*. We keep the coffee warm as long as possible to ensure they can enjoy a hot cup.

It is an act of love and care. A comforting space to enjoy each other's presence and our *pan con café*.

# CON ESFUERZO Y DEDICACIÓN

From the big things, like waiting for me at the finish line of my first marathon, to the little things, like taking me to the park and riding our bikes, my Papi made sure I felt loved and supported by him. He took our family to the beach, the aquarium, Six Flags; picked us up from school; and continues to support me in my endeavors—especially my creative ones.

I've been painting and drawing from a very young age, doing all kinds of crafts. I loved to stack and build with popsicle sticks and make little paper boxes to hold my food-shaped erasers. I loved to finger paint, mainly because I got to be messy. I loved to make collages using photos from magazines and coloring books and making weird sculptures with Play-Doh (no, I did not eat Play-Doh. I wasn't that kid…I was the kid who ate paper).

My Papi always encouraged us kids to have hobbies. Gerhaldy had his video games, Sherlyn did makeup, I painted, and Rene watched movies and critiqued them. Sometimes Rene and Gerhaldy played video games together, Fluffy and I painted or did makeup together, and we all watched movies together. He loved seeing us get along and enjoying each other's company and tried to get as many photos as he could. He continually made it a point to emphasize the importance of family and maintaining strong, reliable relationships.

One night, on our way back home after visiting our cousins, Papi told us:

"I know you don't always get along, and that's okay, but I want all of you to have each other's backs. Especially when you're all adults and have your own families."

We nodded and looked at one another. We thought to ourselves, *where is this coming from?*

He looked at Fluffy in the rearview mirror. "I know you and Rene bump heads a lot and fight, but I need you guys to get better. I don't want our families to be separated and not know each other. That's why I always bring you guys with me to visit your *primos*."

He paused and continued, "Look how Mami doesn't always come with us. Sometimes she fights with *Tía* Rocio and doesn't want to see or talk to her."

My eyes widened, and we stayed quiet. *Wow, grown-ups fight just like kids.*

"*Los adultos tienen sus problemas también.* We fight, we argue all the time. But I want you guys to practice talking to each other, say sorry when you need to, and *mantenga sus relaciones en la familia.* Not all families stay together."

Papi comes from a big family. He is one of ten children and the majority of them live in Mexico. Only two of his brothers, Luis and Javier, live in California. We all visit each other often (we're about fifteen minutes away from each other) and have done brunches, dinners, and parties together. Papi and his brothers have shared their own drama too, but they always seemed to come back together.

My Papi is a construction worker and a plumber's assistant; he's been working in construction for years alongside his brother, my *tío*, Luis. Papi has been a handyman for as long as I can remember, doing odd jobs here and there to make extra cash for our family. His big hands are rough and calloused, built with thick skin, freckled with small scratches here and there and a bit of grime under his fingernails. Sometimes there are splotches of paint. Despite the constant state of roughness and callousness of his hands, he is one of the gentlest people I know.

Papi rarely yelled at us kids, he avoided being caught in drama with the neighbors, he even offered to help them with errands, and he was playful and energetic. He came home, set his cooler and boots down outside the door, and looked for us to receive a hug and a hello. When we were younger, he'd give a surprise tickling attack that would leave us breathless and in need of using the restroom.

The door closed, there was a rattling of keys, and then:

"*¿DONDE ESTÁN MIS HIJOS*?" Papi declared.

Gerhaldy, the youngest, and Rene, the eldest, were at our cousins' while Fluffy and I chilled in the bedroom watching a movie. Well, Fluffy was on her phone and barely paying any attention.

Without taking her eyes off the phone she yelled back, "WHY ARE YOU SO LOUD?"

Papi walked to our room, peeked his head in the doorway, and smiled.

"No 'hi' for me?"

I smiled really big with my teeth and said, "*Hola* Papi."

"*Hola* Shysel." He stared at Fluffy, who was still on the phone. He walked over and snatched her phone.

That got her attention.

"*APA*. Give it back please!" Fluffy whined. "Why are you like this?"

Papi laughed and responded, "Because you don't say hi to me."

Fluffy reached her arm out half-heartedly. "*APA*. HI. *Hola*."

Papi waved the phone just out of her reach and then gave it back. He smiled.

"*Gracias mija*."

Fluffy grumbled, went back to her scrolling, and Papi walked away (Fluffy was around fourteen, and I was nineteen). This is the type of goofy my Papi is with us.

Due to his background, Papi always emphasized how important it was for us to have a good education, go to university, get a good career, and start building a better life for ourselves. He knew and truly believed that was the only *guaranteed* path to having a better life with financial security, steady income, and having access to more resources (insurance, medical benefits, and the like). He wanted his kids to travel and have big luxuries like owning a nice car and having a pool in the backyard.

Papi was born and raised in Mexico and grew up in the same household with his entire family. He is one of eight sons and has two sisters. His dad also did plumbing for a career in Mexico and his mom was a housewife. They lived on a ranch, so there was always some sort of chore to be done and everyone was expected to help. The daughters helped more with cooking and cleaning duties while the sons did manual labor.

Every day, he walked about five miles to school and another five on his way home. He graduated high school and came to the States in his early twenties with his brothers. Once they found work, they saved up some money, sent some back to their parents, and did their best to survive. They came to California in hopes of a better life and worked their asses off to provide for themselves and their future.

He met Mami in an English-speaking class later, and they moved in together. They began to build their lives together (the firstborn would be born two to three years after they met).

Papi made enough to support a family of six, but he and Mami worked together to ensure we always had what we needed. We had nice clothes (Mami took advantage of sales; she rarely bought anything wholesale), we had food on the table every day, we did cool things once in a while (go to the aquarium, the zoo, and places like that), and we usually got what we wanted (a new phone, a new Xbox, or some video games) on our birthdays and Christmas. We were late on rent a few times, but he always, *always* made us feel secure and loved.

Papi and I came back from the grocery store one day and he told me:

"I want you to have a better life than what I have right now. I don't want you struggling like us or not having enough for your family. Take care of yourself, and then take care of us."

I nodded.

"*¿Te recuerdas de Andrea*? Arturo's kid?"

I nodded again.

"She's renting a house *con* some *amigos* right now and has a good career. She's doing good and even paid for a cruise for her parents."

"Oh, that's nice."

"*Sí*. I don't care about going on a good vacation or having a nice car. I want you to focus on yourself, and then help me and your Mami get a nice house for the two of us. It doesn't have to happen right away, but I want you to support yourself and then *tu familia*."

"*Sí*, Papi."

He was the type of person to help others out, but never ask for help when he needed it. He always offered to help his brothers, helped our neighbors with house fixes and renovations, and even invited their kids to go out with us. Mami wasn't always the biggest fan of him helping others, since they took advantage and never offered to help when Papi was in a bind; nevertheless, he continued to help out friends and neighbors.

He never complained about the long days or the endless work.

He made sure to spend time with us, take us out to do something special for the weekend, or even to the movies with our uncle. We had plenty of barbecues with family and friends, birthday parties at the park, and picnics at the beach. He wanted more for his kids and never stopped reminding us to keep working the soil and water our seeds to reap the fruits of our labor.

Papi has taken Rene with him on construction sites on previous jobs for an extra set of hands, and while the money is decent, he continues to remind Rene to apply for other jobs and do better in school.

"I like it when you help me at work and learn how to use the tools, *pero me duele* when I see a young man working at the construction site. Working all day in the hot sun, lifting heavy things back and forth; it's sad. He's strong now, but his back will wear down. His body will get older faster. That's why you need to get a better job," Papi confided to Rene. "You deserve better."

These were the lessons our Papi instilled in us as we grew up. My hands are small, soft, and nimble, perfect for weaving string for friendship bracelets, painting the tiniest of details, and handling small cuts and scrapes. Papi made sure I didn't have to work manual labor so my hands wouldn't get too worn out. He has supported me throughout my entire life and continues to do so.

We are creative in different ways but very similar in our mannerisms. We are usually seen smiling, joking, or helping out our friends. He made sure I always checked myself before taking on an extra task to avoid burnout. I am embarking on my own journey, to secure my success and enjoy the fruits of my labor with my family.

*Gracias por todo,* Papi.

# LA BENDICIÓN DE MI MADRE

Mami always blessed me before I went away for a trip. No matter how long I'd be gone, be it two days or a week, I would always be given her blessing.

*Ángel de la Guarda, dulce compañía,*
*no me desampares ni de noche ni de día.*
*No me dejes sola que me perdería.*
*Ni vivir, ni morir en pecado mortal.*
*Jesús en la vida, Jesús en la muerte,*
*Jesús para siempre.*
*Amén.*

My first time camping (*real* camping, as in sleeping outside in a tent underneath the stars and with an outhouse) was with an after-school program. My friends and I were so excited. We'd be away for two and a half days, goofing off and bonding and creating memories—all that good shit. I had my permission slip signed and ready the day after I received it.

Friday morning arrived, and I got ready. My dad woke up and got dressed to drop me off. Mami also woke up, sat on the couch, and waited quietly as I got ready. As soon as I was sure I had everything I needed (my pillow pet, blanket, clothes, and sleeping bag), I walked over to give her a hug.

Before she embraced me, she blessed me—for protection, Papi explained. After my *Amén*, I thanked her, hugged her, and said, "Bye, I love you."

We weren't much of a church-going family, but I knew it was important to Mami. She had my older brother and I baptized and we had our First Communion. It was during my schooling for my First Communion that I began my habit of praying every night before bed. I developed my relationship with God and only then did I understand why my Mami prayed. It gave her a sense of comfort that someone was watching out for her. Just as she asked Him for protection, I would ask Him to protect my loved ones. My whispered prayers soothed my soul and presence of mind. I felt at peace with the universe and all that was to come. Whenever Mami blessed me, I felt her confidence and faith wash over me, sealing me in love and protection.

Thanks to the after-school program, I went camping with them twice before I switched schools and had to leave the program. Both times Mami blessed me, sealing her faith and protection to ensure my safety. I didn't think anything of it, but it wasn't until later I realized she had done it as a way to soothe her own worries. Anything *can* happen, after all. While I was sure nothing major would happen to me besides a couple of scrapes and bruises, she worried about everything (we're both worriers; I got that from her).

Both times I called her on my way back from the trip, soothing her worry with the sound of my voice.

"*¿Me puedes recoger en una hora?*"

"*Claro que sí.*"

"*Gracias*, Mami. See you soon. I love you."

"Awww, that's cute," Carlos, one of the academic advisors, commented from behind my bus seat that first year.

By the time we arrived in the school roundabout, my sister and Papi were waiting in the car. I said goodbye to everyone, walked over to the car, said my hellos, and I went home to my mother's arms.

---

When I went on my trip to Hawaii with my college roommate and her family, Mami blessed me once again.

*Ángel de la Guarda, dulce compañía,*
*no me desampares ni de noche ni de día.*
*No me dejes sola que me perdería.*
*Ni vivir, ni morir en pecado mortal.*
*Jesús en la vida, Jesús en la muerte,*
*Jesús para siempre.*
*Amén.*

Once the plane landed and we were back in California, I called Papi and asked him to pick me up. He and Fluffy waited for me at the shopping plaza where we agreed to meet, and they took me home. It was late so I didn't want to disturb my brothers, but I walked into my parents' room and gave Mami a kiss before going to bed. She hugged me and said good night.

---

When my parents dropped my boyfriend, Jah, and I at the airport this past summer, I expected Mami's blessing before we parted ways.

But she didn't give me one.

Nor did she cry. Or me. Or anyone for that matter.

Truth be told, I tried my best to keep it together, and I noticed Mami doing the same. I believed she thought it'd be easier for me that way, just as I thought it'd be easier for her.

Once we had checked our bags, gone through TSA, and sat in our designated spots, it wasn't until Jah mentioned my mom that I began to cry.

"When I hugged your mom, it was kind of cool to feel her energy and feel that you guys share a similar energy."

My vision blurred, and the tears fell. I fell into his lap, and he embraced me.

"Do you miss her already? Do you feel sad?" I nodded yes, but my heart knew that wasn't it.

How do I explain to him that I wanted her blessing and needed her blessing to know she was okay with my moving away? That Mami *always* blessed me before I went away to protect me, to keep me safe until I could be with her again? Her prayer was supposed to keep me warm during the Chicago winter and be my comfort blanket as I wept, feeling homesick and alone in this new city. I knew no one besides Jah and his family in Chicago. I could make friends, but that'd be difficult considering COVID-19 and all the restrictions in place all around the world.

With or without COVID-19, it would have been difficult to adjust to a new environment. Unfortunately, COVID affected everyone everywhere and a lot of things were left uncertain. Should I get a job and risk contracting the deadly disease? What if I was exposed to COVID on the flight from California to Illinois? What if I got COVID while living so far away from my family? What if someone in my family got COVID while I was away? There were so many possibilities.

I couldn't explain to him the influx of emotions and thoughts racing through my mind. What if I didn't like living in Chicago? What happens if we break up and I resent him for bringing me out there? What happens if his mom doesn't like me and only puts up with me to be nice? These thoughts zipped past one another in the fast lane as other thoughts took the forefront. I knew Mami wanted me to stay, but I wanted to go out and see the world. Why not start with Chicago? Jah was raised in Chicago, and I've always wanted to see where he grew up, eat the same food he did at his favorite restaurants, and see the spots where he hung out with his friends. How can I spread my wings if I'm tied down by my own mother?

Without her approval, I felt like shit leaving her and our family behind. I wanted to try new things, explore new cities, and go on adventures, but I felt as if I couldn't do that freely without her say so. I wanted her to be happy and supportive of my decision to do something different and exciting, but she wasn't. It hurt me to leave her like that, and not getting her blessing was like getting a big, fat stamp of "OBJECTION" in red ink.

The adult in me was aware I could do whatever I wanted without her approval, but the daughter in me wanted validation and support as I made the big move. I needed to do something remarkably different and life-changing; something that would have taken longer had I stayed behind in the same old town I grew up in and not challenged myself.

I felt as if I was putting my relationship at risk with Mami with my bold decision to move so far away. The adult in me also recognized and understood why Mami didn't want me to go. She was worried beyond belief for me. We had no family out in Chicago; she couldn't fly out to visit me whenever.

She knew no one who'd be able to help me if I needed it, and she was scared to let me go. Her daughter was growing up, and she felt that she was losing me.

My mom's blessing was something I desired from her, especially knowing that my leaving Van Nuys broke her heart.

When I had called her that first time, I struggled to explain the situation to her, not knowing how she would feel—and knowing she didn't want me to leave. I told her Jah and I couldn't afford to live in California, what with rent being so expensive, and we couldn't afford to pay all our bills.

"No, no, no. You can't leave."

"Mami, *no podemos vivir aquí*. It's too much."

"You can move to Van Nuys and get a job here. You're not thinking this through. There are other options."

"We did talk about it, Mami. It wasn't easy."

I told her I'd call again that weekend to explain the situation to her and Papi, and we hung up. I cried afterward.

Later that month, after my parents (mainly Papi) supported my decision to leave, my friend Pamela dropped by to pick up her mini fridge. After placing the fridge in her car, we talked and she confessed to me that my mom had called her mom that night, saying she did not want to talk because she was feeling sad.

I cried.

Pamela hugged me and did her best to comfort me. She told me everything was going to be all right and she was always available to talk. I thanked her for her generosity and kindness.

But then again, Mami *hadn't* blessed me when she and Papi dropped me off at university. They spent the entire day with me, going to all the events they had for incoming students and their families. I saw the tears in her eyes as she left with Papi, and I never mentioned it to her. Maybe she deliberately chose to not bless me because she knew I was beginning a new chapter in my life and she was entering her own, too.

One by one, us kids would leave the house and start leading our own lives. Mami recognized this as the beginning and tried to let go and prepare herself for the inevitable; but she's still learning, and I am too. We don't know how to get out of the storm, but we've recognized this experience is something we will endure and one of many to come. There's no way around it, but we can lean on each other for stability.

At the airport, she knew this was a new chapter for me. She knew I would be okay starting a new life and doing my thing in Chicago. She trusted me to come back, maybe a little different, but for the better. She had faith in me, and maybe that's all I really needed.

# STORYTIME CON *EL CONJITO ANDARÍN*

When I was about five years old, I got distracted by the book section in Toys "R" Us and went off on my own to look at their selection. Mami told me to grab one to read in the shopping cart because she wanted to look at the baby section.

"*¡Apúrate, Shysel*! Follow me."

"Okay Mami!" I yelled back as I looked at the shelves, not realizing she had walked away already.

I chose my book and sat down to read. Moments later, I panicked when I realized I was alone and could not find my family. I walked all around the book section, which wasn't very big, and through the aisles closest to me searching for my parents. I couldn't find them.

I walked toward the back of the store, but I realized how big the store was. They could be anywhere, and I might not find them. After some thinking, I turned around, walked to the front registers, and told the staff I was lost.

"Blanca Martinez, Mrs. Blanca Martinez. Your child is up front at the cash registers waiting for you."

Within five minutes, Mami arrived at the front and picked me up. I was so happy to see her that I immediately hugged her. She thanked the staff for their help, and we left soon after.

Years later, when we passed by the very same Toys "R" Us, Mami pointed it out and joked that they had tried to leave me behind, but I was too smart. I laughed.

--

I always loved reading as a child. If I wasn't watching TV or with my friends, I was reading. I don't know how exactly my love for reading started, but I do know my parents were frustrated over the fact that once I started reading, I would get lost in the book.

It is a common phrase one hears about reading, but I truly did lose myself within the story. I read every book with gusto, hungrily and never feeling full. I read book after book, always looking for my next favorite.

I tuned out the rest of the world, which annoyed my parents because they'd be calling my name and I wouldn't hear them. They wanted me to keep my "listening ears" on, but once I felt that they didn't need my help, I'd tune them out and get scolded for not listening.

They also avoided buying me books, since I was a fast reader and finished my book within the day (my personal record was that I read *Percy Jackson: The Last Olympian* within a day; a couple of hours actually). My parents thought it was pointless to buy me books since I read them and left them on the bookshelf to gather dust. They couldn't afford to sustain my reading addiction. They would have to buy book after book after book, and I continued asking for more; *never* enough books.

I saw their point, yet I still occasionally tried to see if they could buy me a book whenever we were at Target and I really liked the book. (They said no every time.)

We then began frequenting the library every other week to appease my never-ending hunger. But once again, I'd finish my pile of books within three days, and I'd ask to go to the library the next day. They weren't too happy with that.

"*¡No te pasas, Shysel*! How many books did you get?"

"Like ten."

"And you finished them all?"

I nodded.

Mami shook her head. "Go read them again."

"Okay."

My parents never stopped me from reading. They knew and recognized my love for reading was in the stories themselves. They understood that. We went to the movies together to watch all types of movies, from *Monsters Inc.* to *Superman* to *The Mummy.* We loved to watch films due to the visuals, the cool and funny characters, and most of all, their stories. My books were another form of storytelling, and they respected that.

Even now, we still try to go to the movies and choose something we all want to watch and something we might enjoy. We love the movies. We love stories. Despite our shared love for stories, my parents never read me bedtime stories.

They were not native English speakers, so there was a language barrier but there was an appeal in being read to. In the movies and books I was exposed to, a character would mention their favorite bedtime story and share their love of the story because it reminded them of their guardian. I thought that was cute, and I wanted that for myself.

My Papi always fell asleep before any of us, and he's a *very* deep sleeper. You'd have to shove or poke him to wake him up. My Mami, on the other hand, never offered but also got tired from her long day, so I never asked.

But one day, at my school's annual book fair, I got a book I always loved: *The Runaway Bunny*. It was a hardcover copy AND in Spanish. I was so excited to show Mami my new book and share it with her.

Never mind I was in fifth grade and "too old" to be read to, but when we sat down together on the couch, we laughed and joked throughout the story. My younger sister joined us and wanted to be read to too.

My sister and I loved every minute of the story. Mami can be dramatic at times, but she is also hilarious. So, when she read *El Conjito Andarín*, she emphasized certain parts and changed her voice for every character. She tickled and poked my sister and me every time the little bunny attempted to run away.

My sister and I even read along with Mami.

"*Lejos, MUY LEJOS DE TI.*" We all screamed and laughed as the little bunny tried to fly away.

When the bunny was reunited with his mother in the end, Mami made her voice low and sweet, ending the story with a warm, fuzzy feeling.

I still remember those moments when she read us *El Conjito Andarín* and feeling content, sitting next to Mami, her voice changing as she read and tickled my sister and me, and feeling grateful for the moment.

Even the illustrations remain in my memory palace. The hand-painted landscapes displaying the different scenarios of the story are a treat for the eye. You can see the artist's brush strokes and the love and care that went into every scene.

The depth and variances of the blues on the sailing page allow for the child to focus on the young bunny's transformation as a sailboat. His ears were stretched into the shape of sails and with a little red flag sitting atop them. His mother had become the wind, blowing a huge gust to guide her child home. On another page, the young bunny attempted to swim away, but he had been lured by a dangling carrot from his mother's fishing line. The mother carried the fishing rod in one paw, a net in the other, had a red bag slung over her shoulder, and wore fishermen boots. The illustrations were eye catching and full of imagination—perfect for any young reader.

One day when I'm older and have kids of my own, I'll share my copy of *El Conjito Andarín* with them. I'll change my voice for every character, tickle my children whenever the young bunny tries to run away, and end the story on a warm, comforting note. Just as Mami did with me.

*El Conjito Andarín* is my favorite bedtime story.

# FINDING HOME

**"Leaving home, family, the familiar is difficult…and even moving smaller distances, one can feel lonely and sad and lost."**[1]

When I moved in with my boyfriend, Jah, I didn't expect to feel homesick. My family lived less than an hour away. But with the new stay-at-home policy, I was unable to see them, and it made that distance seem even greater.

Even though I lived on campus all four years away from my family, I was not prepared for this. I always made it a point to spend time with them every other week (except for freshman year when I tried being independent and solely focused on school). I made an effort to go home, share a meal with them, and remind myself of my roots, but with the pandemic, I could not go home and see my father's warm face or be embraced in my mother's comforting arms.

My boyfriend was very supportive, loving, and caring during these difficult times and I am beyond grateful for him, but I had a lot of difficulty coping with the new circumstances. COVID-19 had taken hold of the world, the governor of California had issued the first of many stay-at-home orders, I could not visit my family or friends, I still had to worry

---

1    (Susan Matt, 2013)

about projects and finals season arriving, and no one knew what was going to happen next.

Time passed differently, and the days blurred together. I still had a long list of to-dos for my classes, which included wrapping up final projects and my senior capstone, but it all seemed surreal. My worries, anxieties, and uneasiness bundled as a stress package I was stuck with. No return address.

There were many instances where I broke down crying, longing for my family and their familiarity.

**Swiss physician Johannes Hofer coined the term "nostalgia" in his 1688 medical dissertation, from the Greek *nostos*, or homecoming, and *algos,* or pain. The disease was similar to paranoia, except the sufferer was manic with longing, not perceived persecution, and similar to melancholy, except specific to an object or place.[2]**

I remember I woke up one morning with an emptiness in my chest. I didn't want to get up from bed, so I went back to sleep. I did that twice before deciding to start my day at eleven in the morning. Jah saw I was awake and tried to encourage me to get up, but I rolled over and said, "Not feeling it."

He knew not to press further, so he left me alone. I scrolled on my phone for about twenty minutes before getting up. I brushed my teeth, washed my face, and put on some pants. I then decided to clean the bathroom because I had nothing better to do, besides homework, but I had no motivation and didn't want to face my feelings.

Jah joined me sometime later, but I avoided talking and kept to myself as I scrubbed the microwave clean. And the

---

2    (Julie Beck, 2013)

kitchen window and the fridge. I kept myself busy and my mind occupied with cleaning.

**Of course, different people experience homesickness in different ways. Klapow generally categorizes its physical manifestation in two different buckets. "One is more of an anxiety bucket. You feel it in your stomach—it's an unease in which you feel uncomfortable, nervous, anxious, stressed, tense because you're in a place or situation that's not familiar, that triggers your fight-or-flight response," he said. "It's an evolutionary, adaptive thing that wires us to protect ourselves from danger when something is unknown. When we think about home, we know that the sense of unknown and potential danger is not happening there, so we want to return."[3]**

Despite the pandemic, schools decided to continue their classes virtually. But students and teachers had yet to adapt to these new circumstances. It was difficult to find motivation to complete assignments and turn in projects on time, and for some, there wasn't a steady internet connection for their Zoom session.

Some of my professors were kind and considerate; they understood that school would be different and not everyone shared the same circumstances allowing them to excel before. We worked together to create a new class environment and talked to one another.

Others doubled down on the workload and deadlines, claiming we all should have more time to devote to the class. There was no excuse to not turn in work since everyone was home and had nothing to focus on besides school. Extra assignments were added to make up for lost in-class

---

3    (Caroline Bologna, 2018)

discussions, and everyone had to turn on their camera for attendance.

One night I experienced the first of many anxiety attacks due to being stressed about school, not having any motivation, lack of productivity, and overthinking. I had so many projects and essays to complete, but I had no real motivation to finish them, only the fear of failure and not graduating on time. Jah held me close as I sobbed and complained about the unfairness of it all.

How can anyone expect kids and young adults to adapt effortlessly to these new circumstances? How is anyone supposed to get any work done without motivation? Students cannot turn in stellar work with stress and worry constantly looming in the background. Not everyone has a home they can focus in, nor do they have the luxury of not working during the pandemic.

I missed having in-class lectures, discussing with my classmates Piaget's theories on child development; listening to my professor ramble about their personal life, trailing away from the class topic; or even whispering to my friend while the professor was talking, complaining about the class assignment and all the work we must do. There are certain things you cannot replicate in a Zoom session.

**The other bucket is more about grief, longing, and sadness. "The comfort of home becomes like a person you've lost and miss," said Klapow. "You may have some obsessive preoccupation with home and what you're missing, comparing everything in your day to your experience back home, and that can create a lot of sadness."[4]**

---

4    Ibid.

There were times I looked at photos of my hometown and reminisced about the places I missed, most particularly my neighborhood; on rainy days I went out for a walk because the flowers and plants popped with vibrant colors during the gloomy weather.

Small, pink flowers blushed brightly against the yellow-green grass; baby pomegranates with their dark red complexions trying to hide among the dark green leaves; clusters of tiny, white flowers shaped like pinwheels with a small, yellow center; and in the fall, when the combination of orange, red, and yellow leaves had fallen on the dark concrete, bursting with their fierce colors like fire in the dark.

Even looking at photos of my family set me off. A lump converged in the back of my throat, reminding me of my longing for my family. There was the time my sister and I visited our elementary school's playground, my younger brother's art project with melted crayons, my older brother smothering the cat with love and attention, Mami also smothering the cat by hugging her close and the cat looking annoyed as hell, and Papi, who fell asleep on the couch watching TV.

I missed the honking of the *elotero* and the *raspados* and *elotes* he would sell. My sister would yell, "*¡ESPERA!*" and we would grab some cash and run out the door to get some snacks. I would order a *raspado de vainilla con lechera y chicharrones con chile y limón para mi* Mami. My sister and I would also go to the 7-Eleven down the street to buy some chips and candy whenever we'd watch movies. I missed running errands with my parents, like grocery shopping or picking up the kids from school.

**Chansky, Klapow, and Warren all said one key way to deal with homesickness is to normalize it. "Tell yourself it's okay**

**and normal to feel this way, these bad feelings are temporary, and this is part of how change happens," said Chansky. "It sounds simple, but that sends a message to the body that we don't need the fire trucks. Nothing is actually wrong. Normalizing it helps the negative feeling go away faster."[5]**

The lump in my throat settled in comfortably as I released my tears. I cried and cried and cried. It felt so good to release my sorrow and longing. Jah held me close, just as my Mami did. They both would hold me close, giving me a space to be vulnerable, and I appreciated that.

Whenever I cried in Jah's presence, he asked how I felt and why. This is part of the reason why I loved him: he helped me verbalize and express my feelings, allowing me to move on and learn from it. His soft and soothing voice in my times of duress guided me through the pain and longing, and I began to feel okay.

His love and support provided me courage and strength to get through the day and to face the next one. Whenever I felt down or homesick, I went to him for a hug and a cry—and we moved on.

**"There are small things you can do to feel more connected to where you are or you can lean into the things that make you feel most at home," said Chansky, who listed simple steps like having more conversations with people at work or out in public or exploring your new surroundings. "You want to build up your home underneath where you are," she added. "That way, you can still miss home, but you don't feel so bereft because you have more of what you need where you are."[6]**

---

5   Ibid.

6   Ibid.

As I settled into our place, I began to appreciate the differences and celebrate them. In the apartment complex where we lived, the *paletero* came by weekly, trilling his bell to alert the neighbors, mostly the kids, that he had arrived. If we were home and had some cash to spare, I quickly grabbed it, threw on my sandals, and ran out the door. I would practice my Spanish *con el paletero*, have some small talk, buy the goodies, and thank him. I always bought extra *paletas* for Jah and me so we wouldn't have to share.

We'd always try to cook and eat our meals together around my class schedule (and appetite) and build a routine where we could relax and enjoy time together. I shared some of my mother's recipes with Jah, which he absolutely loved and craved daily, like her *ensalada de frijoles*, cauliflower *con limón y tomates, y mango salsa*. I loved cooking with him, and I loved being able to share my recipes and my mom's because it brought a smile to both of our faces. It was comforting in so many ways.

I loved introducing him to coffee. He's not a big coffee person, but he's come to love an iced white chocolate mocha latte with soy milk. We limited our time outside, but we'd go to the Peet's Coffee down the block and grab our drinks to go. He *always* finished his drink before we made it home, and he'd sometimes take a sip from my cup. I loved sharing a cup of coffee with him, but not always, because he'd finish it if given the chance.

**Self-compassion is also key, according to Warren. "People who are self-compassionate are less likely to be homesick and lonely. If you're self-compassionate, you've always got yourself. You're like your best friend," he explained. "But if you're really hard on yourself, you don't have that."[7]**

---

7    Ibid.

Just as Jah and Mami consoled me in my times of need, I learned to console myself. When homesickness came over me, I learned to accept it, embrace it, and then move on. I took in deep breaths, allowed myself to cry, and soothed myself. Soon enough, I became better at consoling myself and learned to ride the waves.

I slowly established a routine during this pandemic: I ran every other day, did homework in between classes, ate lunch and dinner with Jah, and watched a show at night to wind down. It wasn't much, but it was comforting.

I did my best to call my parents once a week, minimum, to catch up and see how they're doing. My mom shared a new recipe with me to try out, and I'd tell her what I was cooking for dinner that day. Hearing her voice was reassuring and reminded me to push forward and stay strong for the future. With a goodbye and an "I love you," we'd end the call, and I felt content.

Although I was unsure of the future and what it held, I stood tall and hopeful. I missed my family and home, but that's okay. I acknowledged the homesickness, felt it, and moved on. I established myself and grew to love my new home with Jah. It was a process, but I slowly learned to love my new environment.

**"With some time, self-care, and support, homesickness too shall pass."**[8]

---

8    Ibid.

# HOMECOMING

As a young girl, my parents and every adult in our social circle *always* emphasized that I needed to learn how to cook for my future husband and family. I needed to help Mami in the kitchen, wash and prep the vegetables, and memorize how to cook *all* of Mami's recipes for family gatherings. Plus, I had to get over my fear of burning my hand and just flip the *tortillas* without using tongs.

I *despised* that bullshit. My older brother, Rene, was only concerned with cleaning up after himself and our room, but here I was, saddled with all the womanly duties in preparation for my future role as housewife. NO THANK YOU, MA'AM. I held off on learning how to cook for as long as possible, only helping Mami with minimal duties like flipping *tortillas*, making *quesadillas*, juicing *limones o naranjas por agua fresca*, slicing and prepping fruit for milkshakes, and mashing *tomatillos y tomates por salsa en la molcajete*. That was all I had in my arsenal when I left for university.

I lived on campus during all four years. During those first two years, I got along by eating out and making use of the cafeteria. Then I moved into the apartment-style dorms for my third and final years because it was cheaper. I literally asked Mami how to cook rice the day before I left to move into my new dorm junior year.

"You measure the rice, and it's always twice the amount of water. One cup of rice is two cups of water." Mami filled a mug with rice to the brim, tossed it into the pan, and filled the mug with water to the brim twice, placing it into the pan. "Add a little olive oil and *un poco sal*."

I nodded, and Fluffy joined us.

"Ah good. Pay attention, *vas a ayudarme en la cocina*," Mami said to Fluffy. She then focused on me. "You bring the rice to a boil and then to a low simmer. And that's it."

"That's it?" I was shocked at how simple it was.

She nodded. "You check on it every couple of minutes, but that's it. It's easy. But DO NOT overmix the rice—that will mess it up."

I nodded and nudged Fluffy. "Are you going to start cooking now?"

Just as she was about to say something, Papi cut her off from the living room.

"*¡Claro que sí! Vas a cocinar quesadillas con pollo por la familia, mis chilequiles, pozole, arroz con pollo, y mucho más.*"

With an annoyed huff, Fluffy did a 180 and walked away.

That was the beginning of my cooking journey.

I struggled during the first year of cooking for myself at the dorms, but slowly I learned the basic skills and began to experiment. I learned how to boil pasta, how to slice and dice, use the oven for quick and easy meals, and thank God for Trader Joe's freezer meals. I still struggled with making the perfect batch of rice, but I focused on learning other skills and recipes.

I called Mami a lot that year, asking her for new recipes and to refresh my memory. She also taught me to utilize the microwave for shortcuts in my cooking.

"*Si no tienes tiempo o tienes mucha hambre, pone el jalapeño y tomatillos en el microwave por cinco minutos. Blend it y pone un pinch de sal. Voila, ya tienes salsa verde. Pero, es mejor si puedes usar un barbecue porque tiene un sabor diferente."*

I've made *salsa verde* in my dorm room plenty of times using her recipe. After some experimentation, I learned I could use my oven to give my *tomatillos* and *jalapeños* a little char for smokiness, add some cilantro for extra freshness, and avocados for a creamy texture.

My microwave did a lot that year, reheating leftovers from home, Hot Pockets, and lots of *salsa verde.* I even shared my leftovers with my roommate, since my parents always made sure to pack me tons of food to ensure I did not starve. She loved my mami's cooking, especially her *mole chocolate.*

Yet I still struggled with rice. I could not get that perfect texture. I called Mami constantly to repeat the steps and tell me what to do.

"Did you overmix it?" She asked every time.

I paused. "…A little. Kinda."

"You have to leave the rice alone. You can mix a little, but only a little."

"How much is a little?"

"A little."

"Ma, that doesn't help."

"I don't know what to tell you, *mija.* A little is a little. Just don't mix the rice. Leave it alone."

I sighed in defeat and thanked her for her help.

My mami has cooked for years and honed her skills with practice and experimentation. She watched a lot of cooking shows and wrote down recipes if they interested her. She had notebooks filled with recipes, her own and from others. Whenever we went to the library to replenish my stack of books, Mami checked out cookbooks too. If she found one she really liked, she'd ask me or Papi to make a copy with the printer, or if we had no ink, she'd write it down. Sometimes I'd sit next to her, admiring the photos of the delicious food and ask her if she would try making it. She'd usually respond with a "No, thank you," or "If you help me, yes," or her favorite, "You make it."

She always tried something new, always experimenting with new flavors and techniques. She even made ratatouille! It came out good, but Mami said she'd probably never make it again unless she had help. I always loved and appreciated that she tried new recipes, mainly because it was a delicious experience, but I also loved that she never put herself in a box. There was always something new to eat and love.

She learned how to make chow mein, broccoli, and beef; she made her own version of Persian salad (which I've made and revamped for Jah); she utilized pita bread for sandwiches; and she learned how to make chimichurri for us kids after we tried it at a restaurant and fell in love with it. She taught me to do the same and to always try new foods.

When Jah and I started dating, I was still learning how to cook, so we usually went out to eat. But I wanted to learn to cook for him once we got closer, so I did some research and gathered different recipes he might be interested in. The first recipe we made together was vegetarian chili topped with sharp cheddar cheese, cilantro, sliced radishes, avocado, and some tortilla chips on the side. It was amazing, filling, and quickly became one of our go-to meals for date nights and, when we started living together, one of our weekly meals.

As I gained more confidence and improved my skills in the kitchen, I cooked more meals for us to enjoy like buffalo cauliflower and Beyond Burgers and learned how to work with plant-based substitutions like veggie crumble and tofu. It was rewarding to see Jah take a bite, finish his plate, and go for seconds whenever we tried a new recipe. I then understood why Mami tried new recipes and loved to hear compliments on her cooking.

To labor in the kitchen, prep the ingredients, cook over the stove, select your seasonings, and have it come out delicious at the end of a long and tiring workday is beyond rewarding. I loved sharing a meal with others, and to get compliments on my cooking was the cherry on top of a beautiful chocolate fudge sundae. When Jah does his happy food dance or goes for seconds, I know I did a fantastic job.

I grew to love cooking and tried new recipes with Jah. I even started to appreciate mushrooms more because of him. Little Shysel would never have thought about cooking like this; she would be impressed with future Shysel and her cooking skills. Little Shysel wanted to hire a personal chef to make things easier, but to have a home-cooked meal is on a whole other level compared to take-out.

My love for cooking began with my Mami. She's inspired me to always try new foods and learn new skills in the kitchen. Mami and Papi both shared a deep love for good food and would always take us kids to eat at new restaurants. At the end of a meal, they'd ask each other what they thought of the food and see if it lived up to their expectations and if we'll come back again. Honesty is the best policy when it comes to food.

I've started experimenting with different recipes too. There have been times when I got tired of eating the same food, and that's my cue to try a new recipe. Mami always made sure to have enough meals to rotate so we weren't always eating the same thing, and now I do the same. Our love for food has transpired through cooking and the meals we cook for others.

When I brought my vegetarian boyfriend home for Christmas brunch, he fell in love with my mami's cooking and asked me to cook her meals for him.

When I tell you my Mami is a fantastic cook, she is a *fantastic* cook. No doubt about it. Our neighbors asked her to cook for their parties, serving her *ensalada de frijoles y arroz rojo y agua de pepino*. Our building supervisor constantly asked her for advice on how to improve her flavor or what she can do to replace something. She also frequently enlisted Mami for her assistance on making *tamales*, food prep, and cooking *carne asada* for parties and get-togethers.

It was also common for her to send her kid, Edgar, to our place for lunch during the summer when she was busy running errands or if her son did not want what she had cooked. He would walk into the kitchen (our door was usually open for fresh air) with a plate in his hands and say,

"*Hola, Blanca,*" with a smile on his face.

"*¿Y porque estás aquí?*" Mami would say in a joking manner.

Edgar would hold out his plate and say, "*Por lonche.*"

She grabbed his plate, began to serve him, and with her other hand on her hip, kept up her sassy façade.

"*¿Y tú mamá no cocinó?*"

"*Sí, pero yo no quería.*"

She playfully smacked his arm and told him to join us at the table.

That first year I brought Jah to Christmas brunch was monumental. This was the first time I brought a boyfriend over for the holidays, AND he was vegetarian with peanut allergies. I told Mami not to worry too much about him, mainly because her sides are usually vegetarian-friendly, and there was plenty for him to fill up on (I also told Jah to compliment Mami on her cooking because I knew she loved it).

Jah's first Christmas brunch with us consisted of *ensalada de frijoles, coliflor y tomates, maiz y pasta verde*. We had a roasted ham and plate of *costillas* for everyone else, but Jah had a very full stomach after eating with us. He was doing his happy food dance, and my parents loved him.

Mami even made him *sopa de tortilla*, with fresh *tortilla* chips, just for him! He loved it, of course, and when it was time for him to leave, my parents sent him with a *very* full tote bag of leftovers, and he did his happy food dance again. Once he left, Mami made a joke:

"I think I lost a few pounds eating no meat today."

I busted out laughing. "Ma, he doesn't care if we eat meat in front of him."

"It's still rude."

"Mami, he really doesn't care. I eat meat in front of him all the time."

"Still, it's rude."

"Don't worry about it, Mami."

Living away from my family has been hard on me, especially since I'm in Chicago, Illinois, and they're in Van Nuys, California, but cooking my Mami's recipes helped a lot with the homesickness. It's helped me gain confidence in the kitchen. I've introduced more family recipes to Jah and his mom, Ife (she's also a fan), and learned new recipes.

I watched a lot of chefs on YouTube like Rick "Sugarman" Martinez, Sohla El-Waylly, and Priya Krishna. I've adjusted the recipes to make them vegetarian friendly and suit them to my taste. One of my favorite food blogs, Pinch of Yum, has been a fantastic resource, providing lots of tips and new things to try. When I remember, I send Mami photos of my lunches and dinners, even when I go out to eat, and she'll text me a "Looks very good!" or "Delicious!" with a heart or smiley face emoji.

I recently began sending my *tío* Javier photos of my meals, and he called me back, asking me to come back home and cook for them. He said, "We need to try new things like that. You need to cook for the whole family, and we can eat together."

That brought a huge smile to my face and a warm, fuzzy feeling in my stomach.

I'd come to love and appreciate cooking, especially my Mami's efforts for cooking for a family of six (!) for years—day in and day out, breakfast, lunch, and dinner. She's taught me a lot, given me lots of tips and shortcuts, but also given me room to grow and experiment with my cooking.

I don't mind being in the kitchen now, because in the end, I know what I'm cooking and I know what I love. My meals are delicious and made with love and labor. Personally, when I have my own kids, I'm planning to show them how to prep and cook meals *with* me. That way, they can come to appreciate the time, effort, and love that goes into a meal. They will understand how a quick twenty-minute meal can be enjoyed and then gone within the dinner hour. Brief, wondrous moments of joy and tastiness won't last forever, but they can be savored. Meals are to be enjoyed not to be dreaded because of how tedious or long it takes to prep and cook.

Even now I do not cook rice the same way Mami did, but I've learned how to cook rice my way. I may not have the same texture as her, but it's still good nonetheless.

# FLING

I knew you were a player, but I didn't realize how much of a player you were until that day. You dated two girls, and they found out. They confronted each other and continued arguing who was going to be your girlfriend while you stood there, not saying anything.

You were so smug with yourself.

---

A few days after my breakup with Edward, you approached me with your proposition: friends with benefits. To clarify, a make-out buddy.

"I know you're sad about your ex, but if you want, we can have our own thing. No strings attached."

I was still licking my wounds after bumping into my ex holding hands with his new girlfriend three days after our breakup. I thought to myself, *Fuck it. He's cute, and we both know this isn't going to go very far.* Besides, you had a nice set of lips I was always curious about.

As a friend, you were strong, loyal, funny, and stood your ground. And yet, when it came to romantic relationships, those great qualities went out the window. You only concerned yourself with satisfying your needs. I had seen you in action before, and you bragged to our friends how you always had some girl waiting to be your next girlfriend. I admit, I found you attractive, but knew I would never enter a relationship with you. There was no potential for a long-term relationship since you always found yourself bored and wanting to play with the next shiny new toy.

So I said yes to your proposition, because I wouldn't get hurt and I enjoyed your company as a friend (plus, that way I could find out if you were a good kisser).

Do you remember our first kiss?

We walked home from the bus stop and sat next to each other on the front steps. We both knew what was coming, and as we leaned into each other, you hesitated.

"Sorry," you chuckled. "I don't know why I feel so nervous."

"Don't be."

You leaned forward and cradled my head and our lips met. We held it for a moment and broke away. We both smiled and went in for more. Your lips were soft, and you *were* a good kisser.

We never told our friends about our fling, and to the best of our knowledge, no one suspected a thing. We lived in the same apartment complex with our friends, so it wasn't difficult to see each other or find an excuse to hang out. We'd sneak away from the group to steal a kiss or hide in the alley and have a make-out session, and sometimes we'd sit on the front steps close together and watch the cars drive by on our street.

We enjoyed each other's company, and our friendship didn't suffer.

At some point, you told me you were dating someone from your class; yet, you said, "Don't worry about it, we can still have our thing."

I shook my head, and you shrugged. I gave you space, and we continued to hang out as friends.

A week later, you came back again. You never confirmed if the relationship ended, but I didn't ask either. We continued where we left off.

Then came the first "I love you."

We were in the alley, and you looked me in the eye and said, "I love you."

It threw me off and I didn't know what to say, so I responded with a kiss. Nothing was mentioned about it ever again. I never asked what you meant by it because I wasn't sure if you were serious or if it was one of your tricks. There you were, the player who hopped from relationship to relationship, never staying in one place too long because you enjoyed the freedom. And yet here was this loud declaration of affection. Did *you* catch feelings?

I had forgotten all about it, but a few weeks later, you announced you were moving. You wanted to have one last moment before you left, so we sat together on the front steps one last time. It was a cool, calm evening, and there weren't too many cars driving by. I leaned on your shoulder, and we remained quiet. You spoke first.

"Well, I'm leaving…I don't know if we'll ever see each other again."

We both leaned in, and you rested your forehead against mine; your eyes were closed, and you took a deep breath.

You said, "I'll miss you."

"I'll miss you too."

We leaned in for a kiss, and you cradled my head one last time.

I meant what I said, but I don't know if you understood how I meant it. You were a good friend who made stupid jokes and made me laugh. I truly enjoyed our friendship. But here you were, once again making a sentimental declaration, and it took me by surprise.

You left that weekend and life moved on. Months passed and out of the blue, you hit me up via Kik. You requested some nudes to help you finish.

I was appalled by your request and said no. You continued to ask and tried to convince me. I blocked you after ending the conversation. I never heard from you again.

--

You came by one day a year or two later. You had a tattoo on your forearm, someone's name in big, beautiful calligraphy. You had a crewcut; a big, oversized white tee; and faded blue jeans.

I was curt and civil in our interaction, not wanting to extend our conversation past me helping you. I didn't mention our last conversation and neither did you. Did you even remember?

Once my part was done, unlocking a set of chains in the garage for your mother, I said bye and walked away. You didn't say anything.

Part of me wanted to ask: Did you miss me? Did you remember the moments we shared? Did you remember the last conversation we had? Did you value our friendship?

I missed our friendship, but once you made that request, I didn't want to be friends with someone like you. I saw what you valued and decided it would be best if we stopped. I'll cherish the good times we shared, but I'm moving on, and I hope you find what you are looking for. I hope you're ready when the right person comes along.

# THREE'S A CROWD

"Here, let me put it on for you," Esmeralda said as she moved behind me, brushed my ponytail to the side, and clasped the necklace on.

It was a silver ball chain painted black with a pink metallic heart and a silver bar that read "FRIENDS." Her necklace was a silver ball chain painted pink with a black metallic heart and had a "BEST" silver bar.

I knew the faux silver would irritate my skin so I couldn't wear it all the time, but I loved it all the same. It was cool and chic.

"There." She smiled as she admired the necklace and her own. Then her face got serious. "You CANNOT show this to Jade. I gave you the necklace because *we're* best friends. This is *our* secret."

I nodded in agreement.

Although I felt bad that Jade was left out, I was secretly pleased Esmeralda had chosen me as her best friend. We were *officially* best friends; the necklaces were proof of that.

---

I sat next to Ocean as Orion taught her how to make the bracelet.

"After you've picked your five strings and cut them, fold them in half, knot the bottom end and separate the strings as best you can. Then you can tape it."

She handed Ocean the tape and demonstrated so Ocean could follow along. As the lesson happened, I checked in with my kids to make sure they weren't doing anything they're not supposed to.

"Now that the strings are separated, you can hook them onto your fingers. You need three fingers on each hand to rotate the strings."

Orion hooked the strings to Ocean's fingers.

"Now watch me. You grab the first string and hook it on the third empty finger on your left. On your right, move the strings up and bring the string from your left index finger to the third finger on your right."

Orion continued to explain the process as she transferred the strings from one finger to another, and I was mesmerized by the movement. By weaving the strings in a pattern, a simple rotation between her fingers, they constructed a braid.

It's simple enough to follow, but it's also easy to drop the string or forget where the string is supposed to go. Ocean looked quizzically at the strings on her fingers and asked Orion to show her how to weave her bracelet step by step again.

---

When I was younger, I loved going to Claire's to check out their jewelry section, even though I never bought anything.

They had a wide selection to choose from. There were multiple shelving displays covered with earrings, necklaces, rings, bracelets, and chokers. There was even a whole wall that offered fancy, elaborate designs for the tweens. They had collections where they had a pair of earrings for every day of the week, a bundle of bracelets in a variety of patterns and different charms, and rings for every finger—and your toes!

But what I loved best was their "Best Friends" collection.

My only quip was that they only had pairs, never a trio. Once in a while I'd see a quartet or even a set of five, but never a trio. They had necklaces with burger and fries charms, but where was the milkshake? Or even a glass of milk for the PB&J set? Perhaps a star to go with the sun and moon? May I recommend a third turtle instead of just the two?

Technically you could have bought two sets of the turtle necklaces, and you'd have an extra turtle to keep for yourself, but I wasn't going to spend money on two sets. No, thank you. Not when I could buy something else, like Pokémon cards or a set of Crayola markers and two (or three) coloring books.

I always wanted to buy a set of friendship bracelets or necklaces for Esmeralda, Jade, and me, but there wasn't a set of three. Ever.

---

Esmeralda and Jade fought. A lot. Someone said something behind the other's back, someone talked shit, someone spread a rumor, blah blah blah. There were times when they weren't speaking, and I was caught in the middle.

I've always been the peacemaker, but their fights were something I never participated in willingly. Sometimes one of them would try to get me to act as a double agent and report back if they mentioned anything about the other. Or they would use me as the messenger.

"Esmeralda said blah blah blah." I said to Jade.

Then I walked back to Esmeralda.

"Jade said blah blah blah."

And it'd go like that for a bit until someone said something unflattering or they chose to finally speak face to face. I'd be grateful once they made up and we could all hang out again.

---

During our downtime, Ocean and I talked as we watched the kids run around and play games close to the end of the workday.

She and Orion had known each other since kindergarten and been friends ever since. They had gone to the same elementary, middle, and high school, but now, they'd left to separate colleges. Ocean told me they were close but had become distant ever since they both started college. They still talked, but their friendship halted in a sense.

As she continued, I thought about my past friendships that ended or became distant as we grew up and moved away from each other. I remained on good terms with them, but we stopped talking. All that was left was a simple "like" or comment on each other's social media posts.

Jade, Esmeralda, and I hadn't talked or hung out in years. The last time we did was back in middle school, and that was it. We still said hi and made small talk whenever we passed by each other in the apartment complex. There was no bad blood between us; we just grew out of our friendship, as do most people. It's natural.

As I listened to Ocean, I wondered how she felt about it. If she had any bad feelings toward Orion or was just coming upon this realization that not all friendships last forever. It didn't seem like she wanted any advice or positive tidbit, so I listened and let her speak.

By the tone of her voice, she didn't seem torn up about it. She just spoke about their friendship and how it had changed. Nothing more, nothing less.

I'm glad she looked at her friendship with Orion and called it what it was. Friendship, nothing soured, just distant. A childhood friend that became a reminder of the past.

---

Sometimes I'd walk into Claire's with my younger sister, and we'd look at the cutesy charms and jewelry they had and make fun of the over-the-top sparkles and rainbows.

I've noticed they have now included trio options for their "Best Friends" collection. I smiled to myself and asked my sister which set she thinks is cute.

# CLASSROOM ENCOUNTERS



As a teacher, I've met all kinds of students—tiny people with big personalities and quirky traits, kids with talent and potential to be someone, human beings with a heart. I've seen their highs and their lows, and it's humbling to see them bounce back with energy and determination to take on the next obstacle.

I am beyond grateful to see them grow right before my eyes. Some of my favorite moments were when I got to see their love and dedication to one another. They had grown up with one another, going to the same daycare and being in the same classrooms ever since they were toddlers—babies, even. They fought like siblings, but they always had each other's backs.

## Sharing is Caring

It was snack time, and per usual, the kids did not like the snack. It was three slices of pita bread served with hummus on the side. I thought it was a good snack, and I helped myself to three servings since no one else ate it (Susan only ate the pita bread, she wasn't a fan of hummus).

Luckily, Jacob brought Hot Cheetos, and in true Jacob fashion, he asked Ms. Cindy if he could share with everyone.

"Of course! Thank you for being so thoughtful. Room X, what do we say to Jacob for sharing?"

"Thank you, Jacob," the class said in unison.

"You're welcome!" Jacob smiled.

Ms. Cindy and I washed our hands, put on some gloves, and handed out the chips while everyone munched happily. Some of the students thanked Jacob again for sharing. He had a smile on his face for the rest of the day.

## No More Math

The kids scrambled to clean up the room before we left for gym. They had an hour window before their next virtual lesson, and they desperately wanted some time to run around and let loose.

But Ben still had an assignment to complete. I grabbed a whiteboard to help Ben with his Math Checkpoint, but he tried to get out of it.

"Can we do this later?" he whined.

"You're not going to want to do this later," I responded.

"I promise I'll do it!"

"You say that now, but then you'll change your mind."

He squirmed in his seat. "But I don't like math!"

"I know, but it's only six problems. We can finish this in about twenty minutes."

We pulled up his math assignment, and as I read the math problem, Matthew looked over at what we were doing.

"We finished cleaning. Is there anything else we need to do before we go to gym?"

"You guys are good, but we gotta wait for Ben." I motioned to his laptop. "He has a math assignment to do."

Ben groaned loudly. Matthew took a moment to think. "What if I helped him?"

I looked at Matthew. "Do you want to?"

He nodded. Ben perked up from his slump.

"Remember, you can't give him the answers. You have to walk him through the problems." I looked Matthew in the eyes.

"I know." I got up and Matthew took my seat to begin math.

The rest of the classroom waited anxiously as the clock ticked. Finally, Matthew and Ben completed the math assignment.

"Everybody line up!" Matthew yelled.

The kids ran to the door, and Ben thanked Matthew for his help.

"No problem," he shrugged.

## Happy Kindness!

It was National Kindness Week, and the kids scrambled to complete their list of to-dos. They could complete their list of Kindness and have a teacher mark it off and move on to the next one. Naturally, the older kids completed the easiest ones first to get it over with. One of the students did her absolute best to complete them and went all out. She made a poster for the cafeteria workers that said "THANK YOU FOR YOUR HARD WORK," she made a "KINDNESS MATTERS" picket sign, she drew and cut out five hearts to pass to her friends, she made a thank you card for one of her past teachers.

While on my lunch break in the staff lounge, Mrs. Robin passed by with some of her students in tow. They walked by and popped into the classrooms to give their thank you cards to people. A few of the students looked for me and my heart swelled.

Mrs. Robin brought them to the staff lounge, and three students came in to drop off their cards. They were heart shaped and had some stickers (one of them had Spiderman stickers and another had pink foam stickers) and my name on them.

They were so precious.

They said, "Happy Kindness!"

"Thank you! Happy Kindness to you too," I responded with a smile.

## Surprise Attack!

I taught a couple of the students how to play Exploding Kittens (FANTASTIC game), and they loved it. It was a little tricky to explain the rules, but once they began playing and saw how it all came together, they caught on and attacked each other, trying to survive and win the game.

Sarah, on the other hand, *always* singled me out and did her absolute best to eliminate me. She'd use her "ATTACK" cards to increase my chances of getting the Exploding Kitten or "NOPE" my actions any time she could. I quickly ran out of special cards and had a low chance of winning. Then, she swooped in with an "ATTACK," I got the Exploding Kitten, and I was out.

She squealed with excitement, and the other kids laughed at my demise. I played it off and told Sarah, "Well done."

She smiled and said, "I did that on purpose, you know."

"What?" I was shocked.

"I make you use all of your good cards so you don't have anything, and then I get you out." She laughed. "Then I win the game."

I blinked and began to laugh.

"I don't like your strategy, but it works!" We both laughed. "I've taught you well."

Sarah proceeded to win the game fifteen minutes later.

## HIT IT BRO

It was the end of the day, and Mr. Kyle and I decided to take the kids to the gym for a game of Hammerball (basically handball but cooler).

I was on one side with a student, Dominic, and on the other was Mr. Kyle, Danny, and Leo. Once the game started so did the yelling and screaming.

Mr. Kyle and I acted as the commentary, encouraging and highlighting the kids' efforts during the game. We both tend to exaggerate in this sort of scenario; add in our general loud nature, and you've got a yelling match punctuated by the kids' laughs and yells and the ball bouncing off the walls.

It was so much fun.

When anyone missed hitting the ball, we'd groan in defeat and yell:

"YOU GOTTA RUN FOR THE BALL!"

When anyone hit the ball with a lot of force, we'd yell:

"THAT'S A POWER BALL!"

There was a lot of commotion, and the kids had a blast. They worked together to make sure the ball stayed in play and hyped each other up. It was so great to see them get along so well.

At some point, in his attempt to do a power move, Leo hit the ball, it bounced back, and hit him in the face.

Fortunately it wasn't a serious injury and he wasn't hurt too bad, but everyone laughed while Dominic was more concerned about getting the ball back into play.

Toward the end, Danny ran to kick the ball (although he wasn't supposed to), and his shoe flew off. Everyone laughed, and Danny was the tiniest bit embarrassed and ran to grab his shoe.

"You better make sure that shoe is on good and tight, Danny," Mr. Kyle said to him.

"It's not my fault my shoe came off!"

"You can tie your shoelaces."

"But I don't know how to tie my shoe!"

"Then you ask for help," Mr. Kyle said as he bent down to help him.

## Building a Community

Ms. Cindy and I held weekly check-ins with our classroom to see how everyone was doing and who needed support. Our kids were hesitant at first but grew comfortable in sharing their troubles with one another.

We emphasized that they should be a team, work with one another and lift each other up. After all, they had grown up with each other and knew each other best. It's understandable and normal to bicker every now and then, but they should always be considerate of their circumstances.

Sarah shared some of her home struggles. She felt lonely at home since both her parents worked, and she constantly helped her grandma around the house. She had no one to talk to. She covered her face, her shoulders shook, and she sniffled.

Susan grabbed the box of tissues and sat next to her, placed her arms around her, and soothed her. Sarah leaned on Susan's shoulder and stayed close for the remainder of the check-in.

## Pass it Forward

It had been a long day, and some of the boys had gotten in trouble. Ms. Cindy and I had a talk with Dominic about his behavior and gave him some space to reflect. Dominic sat at his desk, huffing and puffing over his circumstance.

Danny noticed Dominic was upset and offered some advice:

"I know how you feel, and I know it's hard, but you can learn from this." He paused. "Remember how I always had to sit out because I was yelling?"

Dominic didn't respond, nor did he look at Danny, but he tilted his head to show he was listening.

"Now I don't sit out that much. Breathe and think about tomorrow. Today wasn't good, but you can always do good tomorrow. Okay?"

Dominic nodded and laid his head on the desk. Danny held out his fist, and Dominic bumped it with his own.

---

One of the best parts about being a teacher is sharing these types of moments with my students every day. It can be as small as sharing your snack or as big as working together to complete an art project. At the end of the day, they love and care for one another deeply.

They continue to argue and yell at each other, but there is a sense of community. They know who to go to when they need help defeating the boss in the video game or who can build the tallest LEGO tower. They are a family, and I cannot thank them enough for welcoming me.

# THE NIGHT WE MET

co-author: Jahleel Xhamilton

*My version:*

**His version:**

*It wasn't your average Thursday night at California Lutheran University (CLU): a surprise Improv show was happening, and people made plans to go. Improv Night was one of the bigger social events, one of the very few at CLU, but my friends and I felt that the last few shows were…okay. We debated if we should stay in and get some sleep or stay up a couple more hours.*

**Improv Night was largely popular on campus as it served as a space for residents and commuters alike to wind down from projects, papers, and presentations, to enjoy comedy performed by some of the funniest students the university had to offer. Improv was so popular that not only would students gather in the Forum an hour early to make sure they had enough seats for themselves and their entire group of friends, which regularly**

resulted in every seat being filled (aside from those awkward middle seats in between groups that only the most daring students would take), but students would often sit on the floor and even stand in order to still be a part of the uproarious event.

It was due to Improv Night being such a success that the Admissions Department hosted prospective students on Thursday nights aligned specifically with the Improv Troupe's schedule. When I was a senior in high school, I attended an overnight event for prospective students, and I was delighted to witness the zany comedy that was Improv Night. For me, this aspect of campus culture was a huge contributor to my love of the university, my decision to attend the university, and my overall joy of the student body.

My experience at CLU was influenced four years earlier, on April 10, 2014, when I was a prospective student coming to campus for an overnight event. My host, Andrew, left a great impact on me. Andrew was a Residential Assistant (RA) and got to work directly with residential students to create the wonderful atmosphere on campus that I had been enjoying during my stay at CLU. I asked Andrew all about being an RA during my overnight stay and made the decision to becoming an RA at CLU as one of my major college priorities.

It was Thursday, April 5, 2018, and I'd gone through a long day fulfilling many of my responsibilities. Earlier I attended my research capstone for psychology, the last course I needed to complete to graduate in May with a BS in Psychology. I spent three hours of the day marketing an RA program for my residents in Pederson Hall, a residence hall for first-year students. This was my third and final year as an RA facilitating an exciting, supportive, and safe environment for first-year students. I made a special effort to complete my marketing that afternoon because I knew my evening would be occupied, as I was hosting two prospective students overnight.

Every Thursday night for the past three semesters, I was "on duty" being responsible for checking areas around the residence hall, making sure everything was in working order, residents were safe, and campus policy was respected. I happened to switch my duty night that week with Michelle, another RA for Pederson Hall. This freed me up to take the prospective students to Improv, which I always liked doing to share the experience I got on my overnight stay.

I picked up the two prospective students that would be staying with me for the night from the Admissions Office across campus, riding my scooter, and took them back to Pederson Hall. I asked questions and offered information and understanding I had gathered over my eight semesters living on campus, and of course I strongly encouraged going to Improv.

"This is my first time going to improv since sophomore year," I shared with them, as in my opinion, the students on the troupe my freshman year were the absolute best and funniest group to have emerged during my time as a student. I was excited returning to an event I had enjoyed so many times earlier in my collegiate experience.

*My friends and I decided to go because why not? We had invited our commuter friend who had never seen a show and offered her a space to sleep if she wasn't up to driving back home afterward. So we went.*

*We arrived at the theater around thirty minutes before showtime. Surprisingly, the theater wasn't very full, and there were a couple of empty seats. Music played over the speakers, and there was a lot of yelling and laughing. Students came in from the side entrance with their Starbucks drinks and blankets, and a couple of them yelled across the theater to find their groups.*

*My friends talked with one another, but I felt tired after a long day. I had worked the morning shift at Starbucks that day (there was always a rush before and after classes), went to my two classes, and spent the rest of the day studying for my English Lit. II class (so much reading and analyzing poetry from over fifteen authors…my brain was fried).*

We arrived early to the Forum where Improv was held and looked for a row with six available seats so the entire group could sit together. We found a row with enough seats next to another group. We

left one seat in the middle and occupied the rest of
the row. I intentionally sat farthest to the outside
of the row to be closest to the two prospective
students. I stood up to better converse with my
friend, Alicia, who was within our group and who I
was sitting farthest from. While she and I shouted
to hear each other, I noticed a girl sitting to the
right of the empty seat in the middle of the row.

She appeared to be alone as she did not seem to
be involved in any conversation or interaction with
a group. As my distanced conversation with Alicia
continued, I noticed this girl over and over again. If
I sat in that empty seat, I could talk to Alicia easier,
and I could sit next to that girl over there; but if I
sat next to her, I can't just look at her, I'll have to
talk to her. I walked through the row to take the
empty seat in the row.

*I scrolled on Instagram but got bored quickly. I looked over
at my friends, and they were all talking animatedly about
something I wasn't familiar with, and I didn't have the energy
to join in mid conversation. I looked over on my left, and
there was a guy wearing white joggers with black geometric
pants. They were really cool, so I decided to compliment him.*

*"I like your pants."*

**That was easy,** I thought as I adjusted
myself in my seat.

"Thank you!" I say back to her.

*We introduced ourselves, yelling but not really hearing much due to the noise around us. The theater wasn't jam packed, but people yelled and laughed with their friends as they waited for the show to start. Some people yelled across the theater, trying to find seats or their friends, and there was music playing. That's Improv for ya.*

*"What's your name?"*

*"Shysel."*

*"What?" He leaned forward to hear better.*

*"SEA-SHELL."*

*"Seashell?"*

*I nodded.*

*"Like the sea and the shell?"*

*I smiled. "Yes. And yours?"*

*"Jah."*
*"What?" I leaned closer to make sure I heard him right.*

*"JAH."*

*"Jaw?"*

*"Yes, Jah."*

*"Cool name."*

*And so it began.*

**I like her voice, I thought. It was a peaceful, excited voice.**

**From that point on, the conversation went pretty smoothly. She laughed and smiled as we talked, a complete change from how bored she appeared before just scrolling on her phone. We asked each other simple questions, such as year in school, major, job, and which hall the other lived in.**

**Turns out she was a sophomore English major who worked at Starbucks on campus and lived in Janss Hall. We bonded over our experiences working at dining locations on campus as I worked at the main cafeteria, the Ullman Commons. After about fifteen minutes of conversation, Improv started and all the side chatter ended.**

*He was a senior, the RA for Pederson Hall, and worked at the cafeteria. He was majoring in psych, minoring in philosophy and sociology. We got into other topics but had to rehash them when we went hiking a few weeks later since it was hard to hear the other person with all the commotion (it wasn't a date, but it was a date).*

During Improv, I enjoyed the show, the many jokes, and laughed loudly. To my excitement, I noticed an echo of laughter coming from the girl next to me at the times when I laughed. I noticed she clapped at jokes if I clapped at them. It seemed as though she mirrored me in certain ways, which I thought was fascinating. As the night progressed, I noticed she laughed loudest at the raunchy sexual jokes, and we shared a similar sense of humor.

After Improv, I made sure to tell her it was nice to meet her and went back with my friends.

*He tapped me on the shoulder, held out his hand, and said, "It was nice meeting you."*
*I shook his hand. "You too."*

I recalled after Improv always being awake and excited even though the show ended after midnight. On this night in particular, I felt especially awake. I met a girl, she seemed fun, and we engaged in friendly, entertaining conversation. I forgot her name, but I felt like if we met again, it would not be terrible if I asked for it again considering how loud the Forum was.

I chatted with my friends and the prospective students a little longer before we all went to our rooms to sleep. In my room, I was awake for two hours before being able to sleep at all. I was too preoccupied thinking about what had happened and what could happen in the future to fall asleep.

*We didn't talk until a week later when I bumped into him at the cafeteria. He was working, but it was a slow weekend, so we chatted for a few minutes. I didn't want to distract him for too long, so we said goodbye.*

*Later that day, he DM'ed me and asked if I wanted to go on a hike with him.*

*I said yes.*

# HERE WE ARE IN THE FUTURE

When I look at you, I see happiness and fulfillment in our future. We both have big dreams, but by working together and lifting each other up, we can accomplish them. And more.

*We've talked about starting our own nonprofit to help kids in impoverished, low-funded areas—kids like us—to help them succeed in life, whatever that may look like. We can build and develop a program where the child, their skill set, potential, and dreams are weighed and considered, and then we provide resources and opportunities for the child. They will be given every opportunity to learn and grow, and they might even change their mind about where they want to go. Who knows?*

*I'll be a published author, working on projects, my own and collaborations with others—something inspiring and one of a kind, something that will be talked about for a while, maybe even inspire others to do something similar or with their own special twist. I'll be stretching my creative horizon, trying new genres and styles to expand my tool set, maybe even do a screenplay for a short film. Or I could direct my own. Who knows? Only time will tell.*

*You'll be a day trader, securing profits from the market, and on the side, you'll be teaching your team how to maximize their profits and predict the market's next move. You'll also be working on other projects, like your book and other creative endeavors with your best friends. There's so much on our to-do list, and we'll work together to achieve our goals.*

When I look at you, I see joy and wonder in our future children. I want our kids to have your goofiness and positive energy, my creativity and kindness. I admit I truly do not know how our kids will turn out, but I know we will do our best to raise them with love, kindness, support, and aspirations. They'll be like us but also different. They will have the whole world to explore and travel, a plethora of vast opportunities. They will do great things, just like we will.

*When I look at you, I see our kids running around in an open field of green. Someplace warm with a summer breeze. The children are laughing and screaming with glee. We'll be chasing them around, hiding in the tall grass and standing still to catch them off guard.*

*We'll go on summer trips, someplace new every year. We'll go camping in the woods and tell scary stories at the campfire. The kids will take classes learning how to dance or play a musical instrument or even take an art class. They'll have every chance to explore new interests and try new things we didn't when we were younger.*

*We will focus on family, self-development, perseverance, love, determination, and grit. We want to instill independence, hard work, and aspirations, but that cannot happen without a support system, faith, and endurance. We want them to be strong, capable individuals ready to tackle life, leap over hurdles, and, when they hit a wall, find a way to surpass it.*

*I see myself reading to them at the end of a long day, the children tucked into bed, snuggling with their plushies and their eyes are full of wonder and anticipation. They struggle to keep their eyes open, but they want to know what will happen to our caped crusader and what awaits them beyond the page.*

*I see you placing a Band-Aid on our child's knee after they fall off their bike. You kiss them on the forehead and encourage them to try again. They get back on, wobble a moment, and then they're cruising on the path.*

When I look at you, I see an abundance of possibilities. There are so many things that can go right or wrong, but I know we can overcome those obstacles together and persevere; after all, we've made it this far.

*When I look at you, I see us arguing and talking. We work together to solve our problem and see what can be done to amend the situation. We take a moment and breathe, then start again to move forward. You motivate me to be my best and inspire me to keep improving. I hope I do the same to you.*

*When I look at you, I am reminded of the fights and difficulties we've shared. But we always come out stronger and closer. There is no stopping us—only new opportunities to strengthen our relationship and ourselves.*

When I look at you, I see the sparkle in your eyes. The way the light hits them, and they turn into a deep chocolate brown, full of warmth and comfort; just like when I step into the sun on a chilly day, that's how I feel when I look at you.

# MORE FLAGS, MORE FUN!

After weeks of back-and-forth flirtatious banter and a lunch at The Habit, Tony and I made plans to go to Six Flags together. As a date.

It was one of the best dates I've ever been on.

The first ride we got on was X2. It was one of the more innovative and modern roller coasters at the park. Visitors get strapped in with a harness due to the cart *and* seats twisting and turning on the track, along with speakers placed near your head, for an immersive, 360-degree experience.[9]

There is even a part toward the end of the track where fire is blasted, like the Apocalypse ride, but it doesn't always go off during the day. It does at night, though.

There usually is a long wait for X2, but since we arrived there not too long after the park opened, we were on the cart in about forty-five minutes. It was a great start to our day. We walked around the entire park, going on almost every ride.

But we saved Tatsu for last.

"It's worth the wait," Tony commented. "Trust me. When it's dark and all the lights are on. Wow."

I decided to take his word for it, and we explored all over the park. We got a little wet on Roaring Rapids, we

---

9    ("X2," 2021)

avoided Viper because we didn't want to get a headache, and I screamed my head off at Scream. Just for kicks. We walked close to each other, our shoulders barely touching. I stepped on his shoes accidentally to mess with him, and he'd flat tire me. We talked almost nonstop, joking and laughing while we got to know each other.

He told me about his family, his likes and dislikes, and some of his favorite movies. He also tried to hype up Tatsu and how it was the best roller coaster, but I told him to wait and see how he felt about Green Lantern.

In my opinion, Green Lantern was one of the best rides at Six Flags. The track was set up like a Retro Magic Rail Twister but as a compact maze. Each cart carried four people, two in the front and two in the back. The cart was rigged to carry the cart up to the top of the track and drop—when gravity took over for the remainder of the ride.

Due to the weight of the passengers, it was a different experience every time. The weight determined how often your cart spun along the track.

I'd been on it once with four thin, kind of lanky teenagers (yes, including me), and the cart flipped almost the entire time. Our arms and legs flailed every time our cart spun. There was another time where the cart hardly flipped at all.

When Tony and I got on, we had a good amount of weight with the other passengers and the cart spun like crazy when there was a drop. We both screamed our heads off. After we got off, Tony walked a little funny.

"That was fun, but I don't think I'd go back on it again. That ride hurt my balls."

"Loser," I said, dragging out the word. I laughed and playfully shoved him. "It's still better than Tatsu, though."

Tony made a face and punched my shoulder.

We grabbed some lunch since we were starving. Lunch consisted of a basket of chicken tenders and fries with a soda. Around us, other families and visitors munched on their meals. You could smell the hot, right-out-of-the-oven pepperoni pizza; little kids smacked their lips after taking a long, cool sip of their ice-cold soda, and some parents snacked on their basket of warm, salted french fries. After a few hours of screaming and laughing and walking all over, the food was delicious. Plus, the soda was refreshing.

I got full halfway through and decided to save the rest for snacking purposes. He, on the other hand, couldn't bear to waste food.

"I'm so full," he said as he scarfed down his fries.

"Bro, you don't gotta finish it all. It's only a couple of fries."

"Nope. I was taught to clean my plate."

I shook my head and thought, *he better not throw up on me later* (he didn't, thank God).

We then headed to Goldrush just for shits and giggles. It was a kid's ride, but we loved it all the same. There was hardly a line, and we rode up front. We chatted casually as the cart went along the track, sitting close.

We bantered back and forth throughout the day, being casual and flirtatious, but neither of us made a move. We both liked each other, and we knew it, but there was no attempt at handholding. I admit I wanted him to make the move and I egged him on, but he did the same.

No one was going to give in—until we got to Jet Stream.

Jet Stream was a water ride with hardly any wait time. There were always plenty of boats that rotated consistently, so the longest wait was about fifteen minutes (although one time, during a hot summer day, my friends and I waited about forty minutes). There was a subtle undertone of chlorine in the air as we approached the ride.

We chose our boat, and I sat in the front and he in the back. He took this opportunity to say:

"Hey, you can lean on me. I don't mind." There was a smile in his voice.

And so I did. I snuggled close, and he wrapped his arms around me, never letting go for the remainder of the ride. The track took us along, and we passed by Tatsu and Ninja. It was a chill ride, just us chatting and getting to know each other. We laughed and screamed when our boat went down into a nosedive, and we got splashed with water at the end.

We left holding hands and continued our way through the park. We went on Apocalypse and there was no fire, but our ears were bombarded with the loud click-clacking of the roller coaster on the wooden track. Riddler's Revenge was super fun, but his balls were harmed once again. Batman was super chill with little to no waiting time. (Colossus was closed at the time due to reparations and plans to innovate the track.)

We headed toward Superman and were a little anxious waiting in line. Inside the icy Fortress of Solitude, you heard the carts go *WHOOSH* behind the closed doors. Due to the insane speed of the roller coaster, they had visitors wait outside the doors and only allowed in the amount of people that can fit on the cart. It was nice to be inside with air conditioning after a long day of standing outdoors with little shade and no breeze.

Once it was our turn, Tony and I strapped ourselves in and a Six Flags employee came by to check that we were buckled up. Once everyone was checked, another employee started the countdown, and Tony squeezed my hand.

"All right, here we go! THREE, TWO—" *WHOOSH!*

Superman launched at a speed of a hundred miles per hour within seven seconds, going straight up a ninety-degree track.[10] Once you reached the top at 415 feet in the air, you experienced a brief moment of weightlessness.[11] If it weren't for the (very) tight straps, I don't doubt I would have floated off my seat a little. And we went back down the track. Backward. At a slower speed of ninety-two miles per hour, you are stuck to your seat and cannot move due to the forces of gravity.[12]

It's all over in an instant, and you are released. Tony was laughing his head off, commenting how they didn't even wait to count down all the way. I was still catching my breath.

We walked toward Goliath but made a stop at The Scrambler. On The Scrambler, it was two people per seat fitted with a seat belt across your waist. There were multiple seats all stemming from the middle of the contraption; think of an octopus but mechanical and no curves. Tony and I sat together side by side, with me on the inner side.

The Scrambler took a moment to warm up, but once it started, it got going. Every arm of The Scrambler was moving very quickly, and everyone was being, well, scrambled. The center of The Scrambler twisted in a circle along with the arms constantly moving. Your cart went toward the center and then outward, inward, and outward. In, out, in, out.

During all this, I slid back and forth on my seat, bumping into Tony every time. He'd be sliding too if I wasn't crashing into him, stopping his momentum. He pretended to be in

---

10  ("SUPERMAN," 2021)

11  Ibid.

12  Ibid.

agony, moaning and groaning from all the bumps he took, and I laughed, mocking his predicament.

The ride ended, and we stopped for a moment to regain our balance. The Scrambler really did a number on us, and then we walked toward Goliath.

As we waited in line for about two hours (the longest wait time we experienced that day) we chitchatted about our childhoods, our hobbies, and *Looney Toons*. Luckily there were some water sprinklers above us that went off every ten minutes or so, cooling our bodies from the hot summer day.

There were brief moments of silence as we waited. I leaned on him, and he had his arm around my waist. We were both sweaty and it was muggy, but we didn't care. When I leaned into his chest, I could smell his cologne mixed with sunscreen.

Goliath was a monster of a roller coaster. The tracks were painted turquoise and bright orange, and visitors could see it from the parking lot due to its proximity and bright colors. And of course, there was the 255-foot hill that visibly stood out like a sore thumb. Granted, it wasn't quite as high as Superman, but it was a whole other experience going down Goliath's hill that had you cruising through the track at speeds of eighty-five miles per hour.[13] That first hill and the speed worked together to get you up on the second hill at 185 feet tall.[14]

We laughed, and my hair was a wreck after Goliath. I noticed the sky began to pale into a soft orangey-pink hue; the sun began to set. I casually guided us toward the Sky Tower. I had only been there once before but never at sunset.

---

13   ("Goliath," 2021)
14   Ibid.

The Sky Tower was over 300 feet tall with two working elevators.[15] We headed up and arrived at the observation deck. The sky became lavender-pink, and the sun was setting. From the tower, you could see the entire park and some of the rides and attractions had their lights on display.

"This is very romantic," Tony said point blank. He smiled. "I can see why you wanted to bring me up here."

I rolled my eyes and punched him on the arm. He pulled me in and wrapped his arm around my waist. We stood together, overlooking the park for a while; a little moment of tranquility in a place full of adrenaline and amusement.

As promised, we saved Tatsu for last. We left the Sky Tower, the sun already set, and darkness was settling in. We waited in line at Tatsu, watching *Looney Tunes* play on the TV screens. Tony's stomach grumbled. He looked at the ice cream stand a few feet away; the barbecue stand didn't help the situation either. I offered him my backpack, which had my leftovers from lunch.

"Ohmygoshthankyou." He immediately opened the pouch and started munching away.

"Lemme grab a piece." I quickly grabbed a tender before he ate them all.

"Smart thinking." He talked with his mouth full. "The fries are cold but"—munches—"still good. I just wish I had some ketchup."

We finally got on the ride, and it was a doozy.

Tatsu is a 3,602 foot long track that goes through a change of 263 foot elevation change due to its 124 foot tall pretzel loop, a corkscrew spin, an 80 foot tall horseshoe loop, and

---

15   ("Sky Tower," 2021)

a 77 foot tall in-line twist awaiting you at the end.[16] If that didn't impress you, add in the factor that you fly through this course, strapped in and feet dangling. You are not sitting down, you are held by the harness—face-to-face with the sky and earth.

It was so much fun. Tony and I screamed with delight as we plunged head first into the pretzel loop and experienced a zero G roll.[17] And he was right: Tatsu at night was an absolute must. The track's placement was located in the upper middle of the park, not far from the carousel, and with all the lights on.

Wow. It took your breath away, although that could also be due to the endless screaming and yelling one did on a roller coaster.

We got off Tatsu and realized there was about an hour until Six Flags closed. Our faces were pink from the screaming and gravity change, and we decided to go for one last ride on Green Lantern.

We ran to the lower bottom of the park, going past Ninja, Jetstream, Goldrush, Apocalypse, Riddler's Revenge, and The Scrambler, and arrived at Green Lantern. We waited in line for about fifteen minutes and were giddy with excitement.

Just as the employee strapped us in, Tony suggested we hold hands. Just because.

And he never let go.

As we waited for my dad to scoop us up, we sat together on a bench near the front entrance. There was a long line at Funnel Cake Factory, as there always was, and you could smell the sweet batter being fried and covered with a sug-ar-cinnamon mixture. It was tempting.

---

16   ("Tatsu," 2021)
17   Ibid.

I was exhausted, a little sweaty, and happy. He talked to me, and I half listened, leaning on his shoulder. I basked in those last moments we had together before we went home, and he interrupted me with a soft, yet urgent, "Hey. Look at me."

I turned to look at him, and we locked eyes. I don't know how long we held that gaze or who leaned in first, but I do remember that his lips were soft and a little salty.

# TO THE PHILIPPINES

Paola had never been on a plane before, and this was her first time traveling overseas at age twelve. It was a very long flight, about fourteen hours nonstop from the Philippines to California. She slept the entire time and woke up to her *tita*, her aunt, nudging her awake for the landing.

She craned her neck to see the window, but it was hard to see from the middle seat. Her *tita* saw Paola squirming to see the window and placed Paola on her lap for a better view. Paola thanked her and glued her eyes to the window.

The endless blue sky and a few clouds were getting higher as the plane lowered for landing. The ground got closer, and Paola could see the other planes getting ready for takeoff or landing. This was all very new and exciting, and Paola loved the view.

A stewardess came by and noticed Paola sitting on her *tita's* lap and reminded them she was not allowed to do that. Paola's aunt tried to convince the stewardess to allow Paola to sit close by the window, but the stewardess did not budge. Sadly, Paola moved back to her seat. She did not see the landing, but she realized there would be a next time.

That was where her love for traveling began to take root.

---

Paola and I have been friends since seventh grade, and we've only gotten closer over the years. Despite going to different colleges and living in different states, we keep in touch and send each other gifts on birthdays and holidays. One of our goals is to travel the world and explore the different cultures and history in every city. We are also major foodies, so we plan on pigging out everywhere we go. Food is a must whenever we hang out.

Paola was born in the Philippines and moved to California when she was twelve. She's only gone back a few times but keeps in touch with her family, sending her nieces and nephews gifts and calling them from time to time. We've always talked about visiting the Philippines together because we want to swim with whale sharks, and she wants to show me where she grew up and the places she frequented as a child. She will be my guide, and we can create new memories together.

At the core of our relationship, we share a deep love and appreciation for food, family, and love. We treasure our time together, checking in to hear the latest updates, gossip, and our state of being. We'll usually grab a bite a to eat, someplace new or one of our favorites, and talk.

"Ohmygod, did you hear about so-and-so?"

"Nope. What happened?"

"Well, apparently they broke up, and now she's pregnant."

"NO! How far along is she?"

"About three months."

"Wow."

We'll talk about anything and everything, from the past to the present and the future. Paola will graduate soon and she'll start doing her master's, I'll be living with my boy-friend in Chicago, stuff like that. We always make sure to see how we're doing mentally: how do you feel about moving to Chicago? How is your family? Are you ready for the next chapter?

Our love and loyalty to one another has kept our friend-ship strong and persistent, and we always encourage the other to grow. Our goals may be different, but they share a lot of values and aspirations. One of our biggest goals is to travel together, immerse ourselves in different cultures, eat good food, and try new things.

We have a lot of plans for this trip, and it includes lots of food, island hopping, hiking, water activities like snorkel-ing and scuba diving, cliff jumping, riding a jeepney, maybe parasailing, bar hopping, and lots of sightseeing. Paola will give me a special course on the many Filipino dishes, like chicken *adobo* and *lumpia*, that showcase the traditions and history in her culture. There is so much we want to do, and this is just the beginning.

We will visit her hometown, Bulacan, and stay with her family, and that means *everyone* on her dad's side. *Titas* and *titos* (aunts and uncles), cousins, nieces and nephews. Paola hasn't been home for eight years, so everything will be famil-iar yet different. Her nieces and nephews have grown tall and are either young teens or close to becoming young adults. She last saw them as babies and little kids. We will say our hellos, make conversation, and get to know one another.

We will have a big dinner of chicken *adobo* with steamed rice and *lumpia* on the side, something simple (Paola prefers chicken over pork *adobo*). Chicken *adobo* is an easy, simple weeknight dish easily prepared and big on flavor. Due to the vinegar and garlic in the dish, it is salty and sour with some sweet undertones.[18] *Lumpia* is a Filipino fried egg roll consisting of a veggie and pork filling and served with a Chinese sweet and sour sauce for dipping purposes.[19]

We will eat dinner, unpack our things, review the itinerary, and rest for the next day. We have A LOT planned on the places and things we want to do during our stay, so we'll need all the energy we can get for our fun-filled adventure.

---

According to legend, two giants were fighting and throwing sand and stones at each other until they came to a resolution. They made up and became friends, but the mess they left behind became the Chocolate Hills.[20]

The Chocolate Hills average between thirty and fifty meters high, with the tallest peak at 120 meters.[21] They are covered with green grass throughout the year, but once the hot and dry season begins, they turn into dark chocolate brown kisses, perfect for any giant to snack on. The land between the hills is typically used for crop cultivation, like rice, and two of the hills have been converted for tourism. Sagbayan Peak provides tourists a full, unobstructed view of the land and hills while another hill has been converted into a complex (the Chocolate Hills Complex) that offers tourists a place to rest.[22]

Paola and I plan on hiking up the Chocolate Hills, all the way to the top, maybe even have a picnic at the peak if

---

18 (Yin Low, 2021)

19 (Yin Low, 2021)

20 (Audiger, 2021)

21 (Audiger, 2021)

22 (Audiger, 2021)

it's allowed, take some photos, and then come back down. If anyone is selling *sago gulaman*, I will definitely have that to cool me down. *Sago gulaman*, also known as *samalamig* or *palamig* (*lamig* means cold), is a sweet, refreshing drink very similar to boba tea.[23] But instead of tapioca pearls, *sago* pearls are used as well as brown sugar syrup, vanilla, water, and ice.[24]

We've gone hiking together before on field trips, and we love doing outdoorsy activities. Her default is lazy (trust me, she's one of the laziest people I know), but she loves being out and about in nature and doing physical activities so long as she enjoys it and we can have a lunch or snack after (we'll usually go out for lunch or brunch after hiking…we've earned that meal after all that exercise).

"Here, try this," Paola says as she offers me her *pandan sago't gulaman*.

"Thank you!" I take a sip of her green drink and find it to be refreshingly sweet. "Oh! That's very nice. Try mine."

I got the *mango sago't gulaman*, and I love it. Who doesn't love a mango-based drink?

She takes a long sip and smiles.

"That's good. Still, I prefer the *pandan*." She slurps her drink and chews on the green jelly.

I nod. "I feel that way about my mango drink."

We toast our cups and relax in the shade.

While we're in Bohol city, we will also visit the Philippine Tarsier Foundation. Tarsiers are one of the smallest primates living on Earth. The males average from 80 to 160 grams

---

23   (*Today's Delight*, 2019)
24   Ibid.

and are no bigger than an adult's hand. They are nocturnal primates and emotionally sensitive creatures.[25]

The Philippine Tarsier Sanctuary, located in the same province as the Chocolate Hills, offers tourists and locals a chance to observe the tarsiers in their natural habitat. Guides will take us on a fifteen-minute tour, careful to trek quietly and respectfully due to the tarsiers' sensitive nature. Also, tarsiers get stressed very easily, and under great stress, they will commit suicide by banging their heads against tree trunks. Visitors are not allowed to touch the tarsiers or use flash photography.[26]

One of our common interests is that we love weird, cute animals. Paola thinks alligators, snakes, spiders, and pigs would make great pets, whereas I'd rather have a kiwi bird or even a ferret to keep. Never mind we know it'd be impossible to keep them in an average house, we still like to daydream about having a house full of unfamiliar and rare pets. Tarsiers would make an excellent addition, but sadly, they are sensitive and high maintenance.

A huge part of this trip will involve the ocean: we want to go surfing, scuba diving, jet skiing, and explore underground swimming pools. We will most definitely be island hopping, so there will be a lot of boat trips. Paola and I have thought about getting our boater's and pilot's licenses before.

"I've heard you can get your pilot's license before getting your driver's license," I said to Paola as we painted.

She nodded. "And I think you can get your boater's license too. I want to get both."

"Oh. What for?"

---

25   (Fernando, 2020)
26   Ibid.

She shrugged. "Just because. Plus, it'd come in handy when we travel and rent little boats for the day."

"And then we can rent a small plane for small trips!"

"Exactly!"

The Philippines consists of around 7,640 islands that form an archipelago: an area containing a chain or group of islands scattered in lakes, rivers, or the ocean.[27] Around two thousand of the islands are inhabited, but the three main islands are Luzon, Mindanao, and the Visayas. Luzon is the largest, northernmost island including Manila; Mindanao is the second largest island located on the southern end; and the Visayas is a group of islands that include Masbate, Panay, Bohol, Leyte, Samar, Negros, and Cebu.[28]

One of the many islands we'll be visiting is Boracay. Boracay is a popular tourist destination but for good reason: four kilometers of the gorgeous White Beach is lined with restaurants, bars, and hotels offering a killer view of the sunset.[29] People can go parasailing or take a ride on a *paraw* or wait until the sun goes down and party on the beach with fire dancers.

Palawan is a "slice of heaven," as advertised by TripAdvisor. Judging by the photos on Google Images, I think they're right. The deep, turquoise waters and the lush, green wildlife inhabiting the island is captivating. Palawan is also home to UNESCO World Heritage sites and the Caluit Wildlife Sanctuary, a reservation for endangered animals.[30] They host giraffes, gazelles, and even zebras![31]

---

27  (*National Ocean Service*, 2021)

28  (*National Geographic*, 2021)

29  (*lonely planet*, 2021)

30  (*Tripadvisor*, 2021)

31  (*Tripadvisor*, 2021)

In the Palawan province, you can explore the Japanese shipwrecks at Coron Island; fantastic for diving exploration[32] (note to self: sign up for diving lessons, buy a GoPro for underwater photography, and buy cute swimsuits).

Paola learned how to swim at seven years old, and she's been in love with the water ever since. Her love for the ocean grew from her curiosity and fascination of the ocean. Being in the water brings her so much joy and peacefulness that it can be hard trying to convince her to step out for a quick snack. We both share an appreciation and enchantment with the deep blue sea. The ocean holds so much life and wonderful, amazing, cool creatures that we both considered a career in oceanography. We changed our minds eventually, but there are times we ponder about the possibilities that could have been.

Another hotspot we will visit is Siargao, the surfing capital of the Philippines.[33] While mainly known for its world-class surf, Siargao is also popular for its beaches, natural rock and cave pools, and rock climbing. A guide will walk you through the Tayangban Cave Pool, showcasing the beautiful stalactite formations with a torch, casting shadows along the walls. Afterward, the guide will walk you to a spot perfect for cliff diving. The Magpupungko Rock Pools are perfect for snorkeling with its bright blue, crystal-clear waters filled with fish and marine life.[34] With deep waters and the surrounding rock formations, we will also cliff jump.

The main event of our trip will take place in Donsol, the birthplace of whale tours in the Philippines. Paola and I will

---

32   Ibid.

33   (*PwC Philippines*, 2021)

34   (*agoda*, 2020)

swim with whale sharks, also known as butanding.[35] During the peak of whale shark season, Donsol is the best place for swimming alongside these gentle giants.[36]

Whale sharks are the biggest fish in our oceans. On average, they grow up to forty feet, the size of a full-sized school bus, and can reach larger sizes.[37] The largest whale shark recorded was about sixty-five feet![38] But do not let their size intimidate you; whale sharks are gentle, docile creatures who feed on plankton, small fish, and shrimp.[39] They travel hundreds of miles per day, exploring and gorging themselves on plankton.[40] They swim with their mouths wide open, trying to catch a meal and filtering out the water with their gills. Their bodies are covered in spots and stripes; think of a checkerboard but with dots in each square. Just like humans and fingerprints, every whale shark has a unique pattern of dots, allowing researchers to identify and catalog different sharks.[41]

In Donsol, the whale tours have benefited the local communities by offering jobs and economic stimulation in the town. Whale tours are privately or government owned and ran with strict guidelines. There is always a trained spotter on the boat with the tour; no feeding or touching the whale sharks and no interactions are allowed.[42] Visitors can swim and admire them, but there is no direct contact.

---

35  (*The Traveling Clatt*, 2018)

36  (David, 2021)

37  (*National Geographic*, 2021)

38  (*World Wildlife Fund*, 2021)

39  (*National Geographic*, 2021)

40  Ibid.

41  (*World Wildlife Fund*, 2021)

42  (*The Traveling Clatt*, 2018)

There is no guaranteed sighting on these tours, especially off season, but that is due to the nature of the tours. You are paying money to observe a marine creature in its natural, wild habitat.[43] These tours are designed to protect whale sharks. The tours are ethical and respectful in their practices.

It is our dream to swim with whale sharks and see them in their natural habitat. Our mutual love and admiration for the gentle giants has inspired and added to our love for the ocean. Paola and I will swim with the butandings.

We will get up bright and early, probably around six a.m. to eat some breakfast and get ready for the day. Then we will make our way to the whale shark tour center and sign up for a tour around eight.[44] You rent the boat, gather your group, and head out, beginning your search for the whale sharks.

Out in the open ocean, the water is a deep, blue turquoise glittering under the sun. Everyone will wait patiently, ready to jump into the water at a moment's notice. We'll be sitting on the boat with our snorkeling gear and flippers, waiting anxiously. The spotter is on high alert, looking for any signs of the whale sharks. When the spotter gives the signal, we'll jump in. And lo and behold, there they'll be.

Whale sharks are such gentle and magnificent creatures. They swim closer to you for a better look (they can be curious), but for the most part, they are swimming and doing their own thing. I've heard that swimming with whale sharks is a humbling and beautiful experience, a once-in-a-lifetime opportunity. Paola and I cannot wait to swim with them.

We'll commemorate the trip with matching tattoos. We'll get the butanding, maybe on our upper arm, swimming

---

43   Ibid.

44   Ibid.

upwards. It'll be in watercolor to accurately display the sublime beauty of the butanding. Paola and I have always wanted to get matching tattoos, so this'll be the perfect start to our collection.

At the end of the trip, we will have accomplished swimming with whale sharks and sightseeing, but I'm pretty sure we will be back for more. There is so much to do, and we've only scratched the surface. There are so many places we can explore above land *and* under water. This is only the beginning; that is a promise. Paola and I will continue to travel to other places, including my parents' hometowns in Mexico, but something tells me the Philippines will become one of our favorite spots.

# LOST IN WONDERLAND

When I was younger, I loved *Alice in Wonderland*. It is beautifully animated and full of color and wacky, zany characters—but Wonderland also terrified me.

At some point in the story, Alice decides she wants to go home, so she does her best to find her way back. She attempts to retrace her steps, going back to Tulgey Wood and coming upon the glasses creature and the mirrored bird. She accidentally steps on a rubber horn duck and interrupts a flock of umbrella vultures. She's walking aimlessly, trying to find any path leading home.

Just as she is feeling lost, she finds a group of Mome Raths: cute little creatures with two long legs and two eyes peeking out from their fluffy tops. The Mome Raths form an arrow and point her toward a path, and Alice is ecstatic. She's *finally* found her way home.

She's talking aloud to herself, hoping she'll be back in time for tea and wondering about her cat when a dog comes across her path and not just any dog—a sweeper dog sweeping away the path with his broom for a head. He even gets off the path, goes around Alice, and continues to sweep away the path.

"Oh dear. Now I shall never get out," Alice says to no one but herself.

Now, she feels utterly hopeless and truly lost.

Little seven-year-old me saw the despair and tragedy Alice felt as she cried alone in Wonderland. She didn't know the way back home, and there was no one to help her. She was entirely alone. I worried for her. I wanted Alice to find her way home to go back with her mom and cat, but there was nothing she could have done.

I thought, *I would hate being lost in Wonderland. There was no way I could find my way back if I was alone.*

---

Everyone feels lost sometimes. In fact, it's even encouraged to get lost to gain a new perspective or experience or something like that. Clear your head, and you'll see things in a new light—all that jazz.

While they do have a point, it can be disorienting to be lost, especially if you have no idea where you should go. Should I try to get a new job during COVID-19? What if I get sick? Should I stay home and focus on my writing? But where do I start with *that?* Should I go back to California and live with my family? What if my relationship suffers from the long-distance? I did it once before, and that didn't work out.

There are so many possibilities I could embark on, but it's what follows that makes me unsure about what I want to do. Writing for a career would be *amazing,* but what would I write about? California girl starting a new chapter in Chicago? Too cliché. My life? Nothing too interesting there. My past romantic relationships? There's not too much there besides infatuation and hurt feelings. My family? I don't think they'd want to be exposed like that.

Here's the tricky thing with writing: there's so much you can do with it. You can write an exposé on the latest scandal, a letter to a forgotten love, a research essay on the Big Bang, or even a collection of short stories—but what should *I* write about? I'm not a fan of academic papers because that means a lot of research and doing citations; I don't have an idea big enough for a novel; journalism is all right, but it's not my passion; and short stories are tricky (how short is too short?).

A well-seasoned author has a distinct writing voice; I have yet to develop my own. Should I break the fourth wall and talk to my audience? Should I focus on details and write heavy, wordy descriptions that take over an entire page like the Victorians? Or vague statements that'll appeal to anyone like horoscopes? How do I insert sarcasm without sounding condescending?

It's all about the execution.

(And don't forget to practice!)

I make a routine to write every day: in the mornings when I wake up and in my journal before bed. I read other authors, authors I admire and love, and take notes on my favorite scenes, figures of speech, allusions, and anything that caused a reaction or forced me to stop and think—moments I wish to elicit from my own readers.

I write and I write and I write. I do my best to stick to my routine and write something every day. I add to a previous chapter, start a new chapter, or revise a past chapter. I ask a friend to read and critique my essays so I can strengthen the quality of the piece. Sometimes I rewrite the entire thing because it could be done better from a different angle.

There are days when I come across a fork in the road, and I don't know where to go. I've got writer's block, I'm slammed with work, or I'm in a slump and become glued to my spot.

I don't know what to do. Most times, I just sit there, and everything seems to close in on me. I get overwhelmed, and I cry because I haven't moved for weeks.

After taking a few deep breaths, I look at myself and my priorities. I organize my to-dos, make a plan of action, and take a step forward. Inch by inch, I move further ahead with a sense of direction. I may not know exactly where I'll end up, but it's better than sitting idly while time passes. *That's* the terrifying part, especially because it's so easy and comforting to stay in the same spot: someplace familiar and limiting.

I don't want that. Ever. I want to do something for myself, something that'll bring me joy and passion and invigorate my soul—fulfill my purpose and be a creative, just like I always wanted since I was little.

One of my cousins shot down my dream of becoming an artist when I was in elementary. Being the little cousin, I took his advice because he knew so much more than me, and I didn't know how I could make a living as an artist. I stopped drawing and began to focus on my studies because college was the "better" and "safer" path. While he had a point about artists not making a lot of money, I despised him for shitting on my dreams and killing any hope I had of making art for a living. I just wanted to be happy doing something I loved. Was that a crime?

Now, when Jah gives me an uplifting speech to follow my creative pursuits and have faith in myself, I cry and say I'll try, but deep down, I'm terrified to take that first step. He'll continue to encourage me and tell me stories of other creatives and their journeys in accomplishing and *thriving*, doing what they love for a living. It gives me hope, and I start to plan. My Mome Raths show me the way, but they can only help me so much. I've got to put in the time and effort because this isn't going to be easy.

I begin to write in the mornings before I leave to catch the train for work, and I get into the groove of things until my schedule changes. I have the morning shift, so I try to write in the evening after dinner. I come home mentally exhausted, cook dinner, and take a shower, and then I'm ready for bed and it's only nine p.m. It becomes easier to push off writing, and now I'm frustrated at myself for not writing. I'm upset because I was doing so well, and I allowed that to happen. I'm disappointed in myself, and that's what gets me.

After I'm done crying, I get up, dust myself off, and get back to writing. Now that I've lost my groove, I go searching for it. I reread my pieces and spruce them up a bit, I enter a writing program to help support me, and I change my habits to benefit my health and writing. I make a path to where I need to go. Jah, my family, and friends all help me construct the path that'll get me closer to where I need to go.

I *make* time to do what I *want*, and I push my rock up the hill, waiting to release it on the other side.

My efforts will bear fruit, one way or another. When there are situations obstructing my path or even if the path goes away, I take a deep breath and think of another way. I cannot give up. That's too easy. Putting in the work takes guts. Don't let anyone tell you different. There is no easy way to success. You *must* make sacrifices and work hard for the dreams that are worth it.

How do I know if it all will be worth it in the end?

I don't. *I* have to decide that for myself. I look in the mirror and ask myself, "Will I regret not doing this for my dream?" and "How do I make this work for me?" There are many questions and challenges I go through, but I know they'll help mold me for the journey ahead. Any journey that will change you for the better is not going to be easy. Don't lie to yourself and pretend it'll be over soon, because in reality, it's a long, winding road.

My sacrifices will be different from yours. My path is different from yours, but that doesn't matter. What matters is the work you put into it, along with faith in yourself and support from the right people. Do not allow others to slow you down or lead you astray. If someone does, ask yourself if they're worth keeping around. Food for thought.

In the end, I know my efforts will be rewarded. Even if the results don't come out the way I expect, that's okay. As long as I put in 100 percent and everything I have, I will be proud of my journey. My Mome Raths showed me the way, but it was my own two feet that got me this far. The faith myself and others have for me motivated me to keep on going. After all is said and done, I will have something to show them: the fruits of my labor.

As I walk down this writing path, I come across various obstacles and detours, taking a momentary break to rest my spirit and come back stronger. Please don't forget to rest; it's vital to your health and your creativity. The brain cannot work nonstop without any breaks, and too much stress can affect your mindset.

I've made some friends, and they've become a part of my journey and support system.

I cannot thank my support system enough for all they have done for me. They have given me love and support and a shoulder to lean on when the going gets tough. That's what keeps me going: the love and light that fuel my soul to continue my journey with my head held high, ready for anything—even getting lost in Wonderland.

# TELL ME MORE ABOUT THIS OPPORTUNITY...

One of my best friends from college was dedicated to finishing school. Marlon had some scholarships to help fund his education, but he still had to take out loans for the remainder of it. He lived on campus his first year but had to commute for the next three years because he couldn't afford to pay for housing without taking out another loan. He wanted to avoid as much debt as possible, so he took the train to school his sophomore year.

He'd wake up at five a.m., get on the train, nap or do homework on the commute, catch another bus to campus, go to class, practice his instrument, and then go to the train station for his commute home. He'd arrive to his house around six p.m. and help his mother with chores, watch his sister, and do his homework. Wash, rinse, repeat.

He eventually got a car his junior year, but now he had to work a part-time job on campus. His commute was about forty-five minutes without traffic. Due to the long school and work hours, he'd sometimes crash at one of his friend's dorms during the week after getting off from work around nine, sometimes ten p.m. But there were times he'd be driving home exhausted.

They say driving while tired is more dangerous than driving while drunk, but Marlon had to get home, so he drove.

Fortunately, he never got into an accident, but one night a cop pulled him over because he was in and out of his lane on the freeway. No one was around, so the cop let him off with a warning.

Marlon graduated in May 2020 with his BA, but due to the pandemic, he is now living at home with his family. He helps with chores, cooking, and watching his sister and helping her with e-learning...but hey, he has a college degree.

--

A college degree is the golden ticket to a better life, especially to those who come from a low-income background. With a college degree, you have a 90 percent chance of getting out of poverty, but it comes with a cost.[45]

College is insanely expensive, and unless you're one out of ten people who can afford to pay college expenses, you are saddled with student loans.[46] Luckily, you do not have to pay those student loans until after graduation (six months after graduation to be exact).

It does not matter if you have a job or not, you have to start paying those loans pending your agreement. You may have a college degree, maybe two if you were a hard-working student and busted your ass for that double major, but it is *up to you* to land a job before graduation. And whoo wee, the job market does not look good. Plus, add in the factor of being in a worldwide pandemic.

COVID-19 hit everyone hard. No matter your background, financial standing, or ethnicity, you were affected in

---

45    (*Netflix Is A Joke*: "Is College Still Worth it?" 2020)
46    (*Netflix Is A Joke*: "Student Loans," 2019)

some way. Everyone had to change their lifestyles to survive, and the college graduates of 2020 had a very slim chance of landing a career to sustain themselves.

Jah and I moved in with his mother because we did not have enough money to pay the rent. Most of my friends are still living at home and working part-time or full-time to help support their families. They are risking their lives to pay the bills. Some people were lucky and switched to the work-at-home lifestyle while others were let go as companies tried to cut costs and endure those first few months.

The working-class lifestyle is grueling and demanding, but at least I have my BA in English. I can tutor and edit essays for minimum wage, whatever that is per state, or I can go back to customer service and work retail or fast food. It's all the same.

When I was in my junior year of high school, I remember not wanting to go to college. I was a good student, all As and Bs, taking AP classes and doing a sport, but all for what? I had been told college was the best option for me to obtain the best lifestyle possible. I could study whatever I wanted, get the degree, and work in a career I loved while still getting paid.

But it all felt forced upon me. This is what was expected of me, and honestly, it was not what I wanted. Not really. It was essentially compliance.

I confessed to one of my teachers that I wasn't sure about going to college, and their face dropped immediately.

"Why? Don't you know college is your ticket to a better life?"

I shrugged.

"You *need* to go to college. Trust me, you're going to love it, and you'll have a degree that will pay itself once you start working. You cannot do any better than a college degree."

I sighed and said nothing.

Everyone said the same thing: go to college and have fun, but don't forget to study harder. Get an internship, do some community service, get a part-time job. Do research, present, and get that degree. Interview with lots of companies, land the job, and start working as soon as possible after graduation. Go to work, save your money, invest, and then maybe, just maybe, you can retire early.

What the fuck? *This* is what I went to school for? To be a cog in the machine, churning away as I slowly age and conform to societal norms? Nope.

I remember overhearing that one of my professors left for a better job opportunity. They were applying to be a tenured professor, but people on the committee did not like the fact that they didn't have a PhD like everyone else. The professor thought it over and decided obtaining a PhD for tenure was not worth adding more student debt to his name.

He left and taught somewhere else, with a new salary of six figures (compared to five at his previous). Good for him.

There is $1.5 trillion of student debt in the United States, way more than credit card and auto loan debt combined.[47] The opportunity cost of going to college is exceedingly high, but the cost of not going to college is even higher. Women with a college degree earn about $450,000 more than a high school graduate and men earn $660,000 more (we are not going to talk about the wage gap here; that is a separate topic).[48]

Theoretically, you can work for a company and work your way to the top, but your experience and hours will not add up compared to your colleague who got a BA or masters.

---

47   Ibid.

48   (*Netflix Is A Joke*: "Is College Still Worth it?" 2020)

*They* will get the promotion and better salary, sorry. PTO and vacation time too. Better luck next time.

Ask yourself: is college worth it?

Some would argue there is no experience like it. Your college years are your last chance before emerging into "the real world," and you will meet all kinds of people who will change your life. Some of them will even remain in your life, for better or for worse.

I had a good experience overall. I didn't get blackout drunk, I worked at the on-campus Starbucks, was an English DA for three years, and went on some pretty cool hikes in my college town. I've met some of the coolest people and befriended quite a few; the professors I worked for were kind, supportive, and great mentors; and I became more independent as a young adult. I wouldn't say my college years were a waste because I truly enjoyed my experience and grew from it, but I do look at my loans from time to time and internally panic.

One of my biggest concerns is that society has failed to continue emphasizing the significance of doing manual labor. There is nothing wrong with being a carpenter, a plumber, or even a construction worker. You can make a decent living and get to work on creative projects like a movie or play production or making ceramic sculptures and coffee mugs to sell while challenging yourself creatively. You can also become a tattoo artist and have your art permanently stuck on people. Maybe become a chef and make delicious food for others to enjoy.

There is nothing wrong with going to a trade school, nor should there be any shame in going to community college. Public or private, universities are not the end all be all. People have options that will fulfill their needs and wants, not what is expected of them.

There are celebrities, influencers, athletes, and internet personalities who are making a living without having gone to college. Some of them did go and dropped out or made a career change disregarding their major. They are living proof you do not need a college degree to be successful.

So long as you have a plan of action, demonstrate perseverance, do your due diligence, look for new opportunities, get out of your comfort zone, and have a purpose, you will be successful. Whenever you feel like giving up or hit a bump in the road, your purpose will serve as your guide, reminding you what you are working towards for. Stay true to your purpose, and the rest will follow.

Content creators who are consistent, highly engaging and entertaining, and innovative are successful. Authors who have built a reading community and write good stories are successful. I could go on and on, but you get the point. These are careers in which a college degree is not necessary.

I am grateful for the opportunities my university gave me and for the people with whom I connected. They gave me a space to learn and grow into the person I am today, but I will not be continuing my education. It is not worth obtaining more debt for an extra degree. I do not want that burden, nor do I want to extend it any more than I must.

There are specific careers where a college degree is absolutely necessary and requires even more schooling. Doctors, lawyers, scientists, and scholars need that extensive education for their clients and businesses. Their careers demand it. But are they able to pay off their loans? Some of them but not all. Isn't that sad?

When I look back at my high school self, I wonder how my life could have been had I not gone to my alma mater. I almost went to a big, public university because they did grant me a better financial package, but I decided the small, private university would better cater to my needs. I wanted one-on-ones with my professors, to build relationships, and not have to fight my way for office hours. I needed a space where I could grow and be challenged without overextending myself or feeling any outside pressure. I took out those loans for my education and for my future development.

At this point in the game, I am stuck with my loans until I pay them off. I originally wanted to become a high school teacher but no more. Working in the education field during this pandemic has taught me some hard truths and the reality of being a teacher. I will focus on bettering myself and gaining new skills for financial security. (Besides, I wouldn't be capable of paying off my loans on a teacher's salary, no ma'am. It'd take *decades*.)

Unless you're one of ten people who have no loans, you are burdened with a heavy weight. Your credit score, your eligibility for a mortgage or auto loan, and your lifestyle are affected. Your loans will follow you, sometimes even after death. Good luck to you and your loved ones.

# IS THIS FOR SHYSEL?

## John in a White Lexus

John and I were talking about his past riders, and they got pretty wild.

"Back when ride share was still a thing, I once had two riders, a man and a woman. The man was in his late twenties, early thirties, and he was Indian. The woman was in her mid-thirties and white. I'm striking up a conversation with the Indian guy, and we get to talking about our girlfriends and some minor drama we were having. You know, just stupid petty shit.

I tell him, 'My girl is acting like a brat right now, and I don't want to talk to her.'

Just as he was about to say something, the woman cuts in and says, 'How can you talk about your girlfriends like that? You are so disrespectful.'

And the Indian guy goes off on her!"

I gasp. "What did he say?"

John's shoulders are shaking from laughter. "He says, 'You know what? Shut the fuck up. All you white women are the same entitled bitches.'"

"NO!" I am flabbergasted.

John continues to laugh as he merges onto the highway.

"He really went for it, huh? No holding back." I start laughing.

"Straight to the point! He even asked me to pull over because he couldn't stand to be in the same car as her anymore. After I dropped him off, I still had the woman in my car for another five minutes. *That* was an awkward five minutes."

"Oh. My. God." I say between my laughter.

"It's quite interesting having to act as the mediator in these types of situations. Like, you get some really crazy people, but you also learn how to manage those situations if they get out of control or they get mouthy."

"I see," I reflect back on my most recent situation with an angry parent. She was upset and took out her frustration on me the previous week.

"There was this other incident a few weeks ago with another rider. Now, I have no idea who he was or what he does, but I swear he had to be an FBI agent or had multiple personalities."

"WHAT?"

"The guy was sitting back there, making all sorts of phone calls, but switching codes with every call. He was talking to some lady, and he was talking that talk, sweet nothings and all that."

"Uh huh." I raise my eyebrows.

"Then he switched over to a coworker or someone, updating them on what needed to be done, upcoming meetings, and he was saying numbers like they held a specific meaning. You know, like 2319 from *Monsters, Inc.*"

I nod.

"The last call he was talking to someone, telling him about a previous mission he had completed. And he did what he had to do." I gasp. "What do you mean you did you had to do? Is this some *Call of Duty* mission?"

I laugh at the joke as he continues.

"I'm still driving him around, but he had a stop at a particular gas station and I know that location. Shit happens at that gas station." My eyes widen and my hand goes over my mouth/mask. "I told him straight up, 'We are not going there. Sorry man.'"

I nod understandingly. "You did what you had to do."

"Exactly!"

---

## Jonathan in a Black Sedan

We are talking about my job and the stress that comes with it, especially during this pandemic, and he asks me:

"What does your boyfriend say about the job?"

"Oh, just to keep pushing forward and all that. It is what it is." I shrug.

"What does he do?"

"He's not working at the moment, but he's training and studying to be a Forex trader. You know, trading in the foreign exchange market."

He makes an interesting face. "Really? I was in that two or three years ago, and I lost $8,000. $8,000!"

"Well, it is an Ivy-League skill. You don't just get good at it; you have to study the market, study the technique, recognize patterns and shit, and know *when* to enter your trade in. My boyfriend has been studying for a while now, and he's getting better at it."

"Really? Is he making money?"

"Well, he's still learning, so he's not jumping into every trade, but he's getting there."

"When I was trading, I was paying a guy to send me the trades, and I was making money. But then he started sending me shit trades, and that's when I lost $8,000."

"I'm telling you, you gotta study this, and then you'll see what trades to jump in. You can do swing trades and be in and out, or you can use Deleroan to help figure out where to jump in. Most of all, you gotta recognize the patterns happening every day. Sell high, and buy low. You don't just jump in and expect money. You have to hold some of those trades for days, even weeks at a time."

He's looking at me with a look of surprise on his face. "Do *you* trade?"

"Oh, no. I know some of the lingo, but I don't really know what it means. My boyfriend will be talking to me about bearish and bullish patterns and when the market is low and trying to fake you out, and I'm sitting there like, 'Uh huh, uh huh. That sounds interesting.' A lot of it goes over my head."

He busts out laughing and smacks his dashboard. "But sooner or later you'll be asking him, 'Where's my money?'"

"Nah. I might get into trading later on, but right now I'm focused on my job and writing."

---

## Richard in a Dark Gray Sedan

My driver is an older man, probably in his late fifties. He tells me he's been living in Chicago for over thirty years.

"Other drivers do Uber for the sightseeing, trying to explore and all that. Not me. I know every inch of this city. I do it to get out of the house and talk to people."

He then proceeds to talk for the remainder of the ride, telling me about how he started driving for Uber, the things he's done, the places he's traveled, and the people he's met along the way. He never mentions any family other than a wife who passed away a few years ago and all the crazy adventures they had.

He shows no remorse or grief when talking about the missus. Only love and gratitude for the time they spent together around the globe. They didn't have any kids, but they had a lot of family and friends who they visited and stayed with over the course of their years together.

He settled down here in Chicago two years back—the city where they met.

---

## Samantha in a Red SUV

My Uber driver and I get to talking, and we find out we both work in the education field. She's a school nurse, and I'm a coteacher. We talk about how fast the kids grow up and how much they've grown.

"There's a student of mine and I would have to convince him to take his daily medicine or trick him into it, but now he just walks in, puts his hand out, and takes it. He'll talk to me about his day or something else, but I'm so proud of the progress he's made so far," she remarks.

"Good for him!"

"It's amazing how they grow right before your eyes too."

"I know *exactly* what you mean! There was this first grader who I met a few months ago. His name was Javier, and he was short! He left for a while, but once he came back, I almost didn't recognize him. He had grown two to three inches, and he was more confident too!"

"It's so precious to see them grow like that. Soon enough they'll be reaching your height and you'll say, 'Where has the time gone?'"

"Absolutely!"

She looks at me in the rearview mirror and asks, "What's your last name?"

"Granados."

"Pretty soon your students are all gonna grow up and come visit you. They'll be like, 'Hi Ms. Granados, do you remember me?' and then they'll have their own kids too."

"Oh my God."

I sit back and stay quiet. She looks over and asks, "Did you have that moment?"

I nod, looking straightforward but not focusing on anything specific.

"Uh huh."

She laughs.

---

## Simon in a Gray Toyota Camry

Shoutout to Simon who doesn't say anything or point out I'm crying on my way home.

I was having an awful day at work, and I wanted to go home and cry my eyes out to release. Tears fall down my face, and I keep sniffling to avoid my boogers dripping into my face mask.

I avoid making eye contact with him and look out the window for the entire thirty minutes it takes to get me home.

There is no verbal exchange, and as he pulls up to my drop off, I thank him for the ride and he kindly says,

"*Que te va bien.*" He nods at me. "*Cuidate.*"

With a huge lump in my throat, I say *gracias* and close the door.

---

## Jackie in a White Volkswagen

I enter the car, double check it's my ride and whatnot, and my driver tells me:

"Girl, I don't even know if I wanna drive for Uber anymore."

Immediately I panic, and my mind scrambles to figure out if I need to order a new ride and still be able to make it to work on time. I try to still my mind and ask, "Why? Is something wrong?"

She begins driving down the street. Whew. "Haven't you heard? There's been all these carjackings and assaults on Uber drivers."

My mouth drops. "WHAT?"

"Mm-hm. People will order their Ubers, wait for them to arrive, and jump them. It's been all over the news."

I'm speechless. "Oh my God."

"I admit, I avoid certain neighborhoods when I get a notification on the app. Other drivers too. I don't wanna risk my life for one ride. It's not worth the trouble."

I nod with understanding.

"And then people don't wanna wear their masks so that's been an issue this entire time, but there was one incident where a young woman, somewhere in her mid-twenties, absolutely REFUSED to wear her mask."

"In the middle of a pandemic?"

She nods and sighs. "The driver and her are going back and forth when she decides to reach for his face and pull off his mask!"

"WHAT? She really did that?"

"Yep. There was a video and everything. Luckily the driver got it all on video, and he was able to get himself out of the situation."

"Wow. I hope he's doing okay."

---

## Wendy in a Red Nissan

"Any plans for the weekend?" I ask as I check my notifications for anything important.

"Yep! It's my sixtieth birthday on Sunday, so I'm planning to see some family and friends, grab some drinks and food, and have some fun."

"That sounds fun! Are you gonna go dancing?"

"Maybe, I'll have to think about it. I was originally going to visit my friend in Portland and stay there for the entire weekend, but her family came over and there's about fifteen people in her household."

"Fifteen?"

"Mm-hm. They're staying with her temporarily while their house is undergoing repairs, but I told her, 'I'll come by another time. Focus on your family.' Fifteen people in one house? That's too much for me."

"Good call. You didn't want to go anywhere else?"

"Nah, my ticket is still good for an entire year, so I can visit her another time. I've gone out of state once since the start of the pandemic and it was all right, but I'd rather see a friend and catch up than go someplace new."

"I see. Any other plans besides seeing the family?"

"Nah, imma take it easy this weekend. When I was younger, I could drink and party all night long, sleep in, and be fine the next day, but now I gotta watch myself."

I laugh.

"It's true! Right now, I'm thinking of going for a nice dinner with my friends and drink some wine tonight, see some family on Saturday and go to the mall, and then go dancing on Sunday night."

"That sounds fun. I hope you enjoy yourself."

"Thank you! Although I could just take myself out, dress up, and go to a bar someplace lively. You know, just enjoy the atmosphere and talk to a stranger."

"Really? Wouldn't you rather bring a friend and just hang out?"

"I could do that, but sometimes it's nice to be by yourself. Do something different, and who knows, maybe I'll meet someone new and have a thoughtful conversation."

---

## Ben in a Black Subaru

After making a U-turn to correct the wrong turn from earlier, Ben apologizes for his driving.

"I'm talking too much and not focusing on the driving, haha," he explained.

"No worries, I still have enough time to make it to work on time," I respond.

We talk, asking the usual questions: where am I from, what do I do, when did he start driving for Uber, where is he from, etc. He has a gentle, kind voice with a jokey side to him.

"You look so young. How old are you?"

"Twenty-three."

"Ah, okay. What do you do outside of work? For fun?"

"I like to go out and eat at new places, I like to relax at home, or go to the lake. I just went to the lake last weekend for the first time, and I loved it. The water was so calm and peaceful and my boyfriend and I were eating dinner together—"

"Oh, don't feel like I'm going to ask you out or anything. I'm past that age." He chuckles.

I laugh. "You're all good. I didn't get that feeling at all."

"Maybe if I was thirty, forty years younger, *then* I'd try, but—" He laughs and his shoulders shake from the laughter. "I'm seventy-five years old, I'm way past that age."

I bust out laughing.

"Besides, that isn't my style. This is how I used to do it, back then when I was a young buck: I'd walk up to a young lady and ask a question. Something light and casual, to get the conversation going. Then I'd compliment her, something small like her shirt brings out the color in her eyes."

"That's cute."

He looks at me in the rearview. "Ah, but you see, I'm bringing attention that I notice the little things like that."

"Ah, I see!"

He nods. "Now you get it. I'm winning her over with my wits AND charm. I can keep the conversation going, get her talking about herself, and then I ask her if she's willing to go on a date. It worked almost every time. They only said no if they were seeing someone."

"Wow. Did you teach your sons your technique?" I smile.

"Of course! And they were able to land the girl they wanted."

"Nice!"

---

## Steve in a Gray Honda Accord

My Uber driver is a professionally certified matchmaker and has been for over fifteen years. He loves my attitude and way of speaking; the way I carry myself made a good impression. And yes, he asks if I am in the market. I politely tell him I'm committed to someone.

We chat about the type of clients he works with and the type who make for good matches.

"I look for the cream of the crop. I single out the junkies and toss them aside. There is no point in working with them if they won't work with me. If you cannot text me back consistently and within a timely manner, you are not ready for commitment."

He even gives me his promo flyer, *just in case* I know anyone thinking of being set up or if I ever do become free.

"By the way you talk, you can infer about your attitude, and it's very promising. I know a couple of my clients who would be a good match for you."

"What do you look for when matching your clients?"

"*Everything,* but I mostly match them based on if they are a good person. If they are good at communicating with me, their morals and values are good, and if they are willing to commit."

"Do you match people based on culture or ethnicity?"

"I match people from all sorts of different backgrounds. So long as they match in my eyes, based on my evaluations, they're good."

He has a very high success rate, about 97 percent. Out of the seventy-two people he's worked with in the past year, only eight pairings have broken up. Eight.

"Do you know the three main causes of divorce? Try to guess."

"Financials." I say confidently.

"Ninety percent of divorces happen because of financials. Very good. What's another one?"

"Disloyalty?"

He looks at me in the rearview mirror. "Misunderstandings."

"Oh! And miscommunication."

"Misunderstandings and miscommunication are the other two big deal breakers. Misunderstandings happen when you don't text or call back. That's why I toss out the junkies in the beginning because they are clearly not ready. Miscommunication happens when couples speak out of anger or an intense emotion. You say something that you regret, or you don't give your partner space to reflect. Never speak to your partner until you've cooled down. Give each other that space."

I nod. I immediately think of all the times I asked Jah to give me space when I was very upset or needed time to sort my feelings *before* we came to a solution. And then he says:

"Another thing you can do right now to ensure your relationship endures is first: tell your partner you love them about five times a day. Every day. Create a situation in which you can say 'I love you' or show your appreciation for them. Second thing: kiss them. Every day. Kiss them to say thank you and kiss them goodbye and hello. Don't go a day without giving them a kiss."

I beam with understanding and a little bit of pride. Jah and I do that already—we have for the past three years. I think of a particular incident in which we were talking, and I kissed him on the nose out of nowhere. He asked me, "What made you do that?"

I paused for a moment and said, "I'm naturally affectionate and we both know this, but there was no real reason…I think it's come to the point where I just kinda do it on autopilot. I see you, and I want to kiss you, you know?"

He nodded. "Me too."

# BIG GIRLS DON'T CRY

My back was against the wall and Esmeralda said to me pointedly:

"I used to be just like you, but then I got mean. I had to learn to stand up for myself and grow up. I remember being that little girl, and I cry for her. I miss being that little girl."

I was eight years old, and she was nine.

--

Ever since I was a little girl, I'd been told I'm "too nice" and needed to be "meaner." I needed to stand up for myself. While they did have a point about me speaking up, I never wanted to be mean. I didn't want to be that bitch.

But as I grew up, I learned to tease and crack jokes that were a little hurtful. In my group of friends, that's all we did. We all poked and prodded at each other's insecurities. Don't get me wrong, we all loved and cared for one another, but we picked at each other's scabs constantly, never letting them fully heal.

My best friend Paola and I rarely let our guards down. I've only ever seen her cry once. I wonder if she felt exposed when the little girl in her cried openly.

I know I did when Genesis saw me cry. I don't *ever* cry, especially not in public. I saw it as an admission of defeat—that I wasn't strong enough to maintain my composure. After all, hadn't I felt the need to be stronger? That I had to build this façade of being independent and not needing help from others?

My high school self thought it best to deal with my problems on my own and to repress my feelings to be "tough" and "independent." I thought I had to be strong and stand on my own to weather any storm that came my way. What I didn't realize was that it was so exhausting to do it all by myself. Genesis saw through my bullshit. Thank God she did, or else I would have fallen apart.

"Look, I know that you put up this act to look tough, but there's no need to. You can always come to me for help. I don't want you to ever feel like you're alone. You're not. We're here for you. *I'm* here for you."

I started to cry, and while I hated it, my heart felt lighter from the release. I sniffled loudly and wiped my face with my sleeve. "It's just…hard, ya know?" The little girl didn't know what to say or how to describe the feelings after being silenced for so long, but she was grateful for this opportunity.

She nodded in agreement. "I know." She reached out to hug me, and I let her.



My current friends will tell you I am honest—"brutally honest," as my ex-best friend put it once. I try to not hold back because I want to share *my* truth and *my* feelings. It can be upsetting at times.

Jeanett and I don't hold back from one another. I love her for that. We gossip, talk shit, and joke with one another every time we get together. *A las mujeres les encanta a chismear.*

"Well, someone had to say it," she said as we reflected on a past drama.

"Thank God you did." I laugh. "I couldn't after all *that.* She wouldn't have responded well to me" (we were talking about my ex-best friend).

I will either say nothing or say what I feel. I don't ever want to hold back, but my past dramas have taught me that silence is just as crucial. Sometimes, you must see what the other person holds back; let them say their piece and then decide if you want to share yours.

My current friendships have taught me to be protective and understanding of my friends. My childhood friendships have either endured or gone out; we've grown up and moved on, healing ourselves and our past traumas. Some friendships aren't meant to last forever, but they can teach us things.

They teach us to treasure the happy moments—the ones where you laugh so hard you pee your pants or soda comes out of your nose, when you hype each other up before a big event, when you're in the car singing along to the music at the top of your lungs, or enjoying each other's company in silence—and to endure the difficult moments, like consoling each other after a breakup, when parents are going through a divorce, or soothing the other during an anxiety attack. We see the good and the bad sides of each other yet encourage the other to do better and help them see how to move on.

I am exhausted. This balancing act of being tough and soft is difficult and taxing on my being. There are days when I don't want to be both, but I do it anyway with a smile on my face and my walls up. The little girl has learned to be protective yet still looks for kindness in everyone.

I laugh loudly and poke fun in retaliation of a comment directed at me. Am I taking it personally? Perhaps, but if you laugh it off with a smirk, maybe they won't notice; or roll your eyes just like you practiced with your sister.

On the other hand, I yield to my gentler nature—my soft and welcoming compassion. I listen quietly and offer comfort with my words in times of need. I ask questions to guide them in their uncertainty and emotional fog.

Yet, I stay true to myself, an open hearth for those who are weary and need warmth; stand too close to the fire and you'll get burned. My fire burns bright and brilliant, crackling loudly in the stone fireplace.

My softness is something I have cultivated and maintained throughout the years. The little girl has grown up yet remains hopeful that others can choose to be kind and compassionate, just as she continues to do. My toughness is something I had to learn, but I am grateful for that edge. It enhances my softness and provides brutal honesty when needed with an attentive ear and forgiving heart—a welcoming hearth for you to visit whenever, so long as you don't squander my flame.

—

When Yesika Salgado popped up on my Instagram feed, I was intrigued. She is a Salvadoran poet who writes about her childhood, growing up in LA, and her experience being a woman of color.

She had written her book *Corazón* not too long ago, and I remember wanting to read it but I had no money at the time. I instead heard her spoken piece, "State of Mind: Finding My Therapist of Color."

As she stood there and spoke her piece, I marveled at how she phrased the confusion and pain she felt being a woman of color; admitted being soft and "too much." My eyes began to fill about halfway, and once she was done, I cried.

There was so much she touched upon in under three minutes. The emotion she put into her words I felt in every pulse of my heart. Her soft voice carried so much weight from all the pain and confusion she's experienced. She emphasized certain sounds in a word, highlighting the stops and pauses in every line. It moved me.

The little girl inside me felt seen. My fire burned brighter.

# ACKNOWLEDGMENTS

Special thanks to:

MY FAMILY

Thank you for providing a loving, caring home filled with laughter, stories, jokes, *chisme*, food, and inspiration. *Te quiero mucho.*

LEE CASSIDY

Thank you for being the first person to edit and critique my essays. I am indebted to you and our friendship. I cannot wait to see you shine bright when your time comes.

ZEESHAN ALI

Thank you for referring me to Creators Institute and being a wonderful mentor. I know I don't always make the best decisions, but thank you for believing in me and supporting me (and for treating me to lunch).

MY NDP TEAM

Thank you for your support, your advice, helping me publish *cafecito*, and helping me transform my dream into reality.

Thank you to the Cover Design Team for that gorgeous cover and understanding my vision. And a very special shoutout to Kyra Ann Dawkins, Melody Delgado Lorbeer, and Katherine Mazoyer for your guidance. And finally,

JAHLEEL XHAMILTON
My darling sunny boi, you have done so much for me. The love and gratitude I have for you is impossible to convey through words. I can only pray we have enough time to fulfill our dreams together. *Te amo con todo mi corazón.*

---

I also want to take a moment and thank everyone who supported me on my *cafecito* journey. Thank you for joining my community. I could not have done this without your help. I am beyond grateful for your love and support for *cafecito.* I cannot wait to share more of my story with you.

*Gracias por tu apoyo.*

LESLIE ALEXANDER
JESSI VAN DER LAAN
ALEXYZ VALDES
LEE CASSIDY
MARIE E. RODRIGUEZ
MELISSA CARR
MARIANCE BAYLEN
KAZEEM TIJANI

SHERLYN GRANADOS
PATRICIA YANTZER
TINATHY TRAN
ANA CORDOBA
JENNIFER ASHER
CASSANDRA NAVA
KAILEY WALTERS
MAHAM KAZMI
CYNTHIA DUARTE
JOSE SERRANO
VALERIA GARCIA
DANIELA GUTIERREZ
ANTHONY LOPEZ
MOLLY DODSON
JOSIAH LEDOUX-HAYES
ADAM LEMKE-BELL
KELLY O'BRIEN
CARLOS GUERRERO
JASON GARCIA
ERIK WALLER
PAMELA HERNANDEZ
SARAH CARTER
JOSEPHINE RODRIGUEZ
RENE GRANADOS
JASMIN NEVAREZ
GRACE KWAK
HALEY NEWLIN
GENESIS ABRAHAM
ABIGAIL ESPINOZA
ENGELBER RUIZ

RITA KYURKLYAN

VALERIA ALOE

SANG LEE

MARISOL RUIZ

HARRISON RUUD

KAITLYN HARLOW

KAREN HERNANDEZ

JACOB CARNOWELL

NORA KOMAI

KARLA BANEGAS

JOHANNES LUNA

JOSE PEREZ

BEAR ABUBO

KRISHNARAO NANDIPATI

SNIGDHA NANDIPATI

PAOLA PEREZ

ANDREA MEDINA

MARCO RODRIGUEZ

ARIANA LATIFI

MARLON RODRIGUEZ

SAMUEL DILLOW

ERIC KOESTER

JEANETT FAYED

CASSIDY CRAVEN

MAYRA SALOMON

JOANNA BURNS

LI BLOOM

NZINGA-AIN BARBEROUSSE

SYDNEY STEANS-GAIL

TANIA HUERTA

REESE COULTER
CLAUDIA MARTINEZ
SONJA CRUM KNIGHT
STEPHANY MARTÍNEZ
ERIK HUERTA
ERNESTO J. GRANADOS
JOSÉ LUIS GRANADOS
LAURA MONSREAL
BELA MOTÉ
KRISTEN CASE
CHRISTTAG VASQUEZ
SUSAN DONATO

# APPENDIX

## Chapter 6: Finding Home


- Beck, Julie. "When Nostalgia Was a Disease." *The Atlantic*, Atlantic Media Company, August 14, 2013. Accessed March 15, 2020. www.theatlantic.com/health/archive/2013/08/when-nostalgia-was-a-disease/278648/.

- Bologna, Caroline. "What Happens to Your Body When You Feel Homesick." *HuffPost*, June 27, 2018. Accessed March 15, 2020. www.huffpost.com/entry/what-happens-mind-body-homesick_n_5b201ebde4b09d7a3d77eee1.

- *TEDx Talks.* "A History of Homesickness." May 30, 2013. Video, 13:22. https://www.youtube.com/watch?v=6WjzhuF-pNDc.


## Chapter 13: More Flags, More Fun!


- Six Flags Magic Mountain. "Goliath." Ride Information. Accessed March 20, 2021. https://www.sixflags.com/magic-mountain/attractions/goliath-2.

- Six Flags Magic Mountain. "SUPERMAN: Escape from Krypton." Ride Information. Accessed March 20, 2021. https://

www.sixflags.com/magicmountain/attractions/superman-escape-krypton.


- Six Flags Magic Mountain. "Tatsu." Ride Information. Accessed March 20, 2021. https://www.sixflags.com/magicmountain/attractions/tatsu.

- Six Flags Magic Mountain. "X2." Ride Information. Accessed March 20, 2021. https://www.sixflags.com/magicmountain/attractions/x2-coaster.

- Worden, Leon. "Sky Tower Construction." scvhistory.com. 2012. https://scvhistory.com/scvhistory/mm0100.htm. Accessed March 20, 2021.


## Chapter 14: To the Philippines


- Audiger, Stephan. "15 Best Things to Do in Bohol Island." *Hotels.com*, www.hotels.com/go/philippines/best-bohol-island-things-to-do. Accessed 11 April 2021.

- Audiger, Stephan. "The Chocolate Hills." *Hotels.com*, https://www.hotels.com/go/philippines/chocolate-hills. Accessed 11 April 2021.

- "Boracay." *lonely planet*. https://www.lonelyplanet.com/philippines/the-visayas/boracay. Accessed 11 April 2021.

- "Calauit Wildlife Sanctuary." *Tripadvisor*. www.tripadvisor.com/Attraction_Review-g1642824-d2068191-Reviews-Calauit_Wildlife_Sanctuary-Busuanga_Island_Palawan_Province_Mimaropa.html. Accessed May 29, 2021.

- David, Samantha. "Where to Dive Ethically with Whale Sharks in the Philippines." *smile.* 16 November 2021. smile.cebupacificair.com/dive-ethically-whale-sharks-philippines/. Accessed 15 May 2021.

- "Easy Sago Gulaman (Samalamig or Palamig)." *Today's Delight.* September 17, 2019. www.todaysdelight.com/sago-gulaman/. Accessed May 15, 2021.

- "Explore Palawan Island." *Tripadvisor.* www.tripadvisor.com/Tourism-g294255-Palawan_Island_Palawan_Province_Mimaropa-Vacations.html. Accessed 11 April 2021.

- Fernando, Cielo. "Philippine Tarsier Sanctuary: A Place Devoted to Saving the Lives of the Emotionally-Sensitive Species." *ZENROOMS.* April 29, 2020. www.zenrooms.com/blog/post/philippine-tarsier-sanctuary/. Accessed 23 May 2021.

- "Know Before You Go: the Philippines." *National Geographic.* www.nationalgeographic.com/travel/article/partner-content-know-before-you-go-the-philippines. Accessed 15 May 2021.

- "Lechon or Roasted Pig." *Philippine National Symbols.* sites.google.com/site/philippinenationalsymbols/philippine-national-dish.

- "Siargao." *PwC Philippines.* https://www.pwc.com/ph/en/gems/siargao.html. Accessed 11 April 2021.

- "Things to Do in Siargao Island Philippines." *agoda.* 9 July 2020. www.agoda.com/travel-guides/philippines/siargao-island/things-to-do-in-siargao-island-philippines-top-activities-attractions?cid=1844104. Accessed 15 May 2021.

- *The Traveling Clatt.* "Whale Sharks in the Philippines: Everything You Need to Know." March 21 2018. Video. 30:27. https://www.youtube.com/watch?v=97LNH-pzmq8.

- "Whale Sharks." *National Geographic.* www.nationalgeographic.com/animals/fish/facts/whale-shark. Accessed 2021.

- "Whale Sharks in Donsol." *Ultimate Shark Diving.* www.sharkdivingphilippines.com/whalesharks.html. Accessed 23 May 2021.

- "Whale Shark: Facts." *WorldWildlifeFund.* www.worldwildlife.org/species/whale-shark. Accessed May 23, 2021.

- "What is an Archipelago?." *National Ocean Service,* oceanservice.noaa.gov/facts/archipelago.html. Accessed 23 May 2021.

- Yin Low, Bee. "Chicken Adobo." *Rasa Malaysia,* https://rasamalaysia.com/classic-chicken-adobo-recipe/. Accessed 15 May 2021.

- Yin Low, Bee. "Lumpia (Filipino Spring Rolls)." *Rasa Malaysia,* https://rasamalaysia.com/lumpia-filipino-spring-rolls-recipe/. Accessed 15 May 2021.

## Chapter 16: Tell Me More About This Opportunity...

- *Netflix Is A Joke.* "Is College Still Worth it? | Patriot Act with Hasan Minhaj." June 15, 2020. Video, 21:26. https://www.youtube.com/watch?v=YytF2v7Vvwo.

- *Netflix Is A Joke.* "Student Loans | Patriot Act with Hasan Minhaj." February 24, 2019. Video, 27:31. https://www.youtube.com/watch?v=toCyBv18A5k.